Author biography

I am Hemilkumar P Patel. Who is mommy and daddy? The mother father of a son or daughter, So I want to send them a message. You people also take my point forward.

This is one of the things I wrote that I put in front of you in the form of a story. It happens that those who do timepass always break the heart of others and say that love like Krishna Radha. Understand that Krishna and Radha love each other, not like you, one playwright breaks one. They were both one. If Krishna is walking then the shadow falls on Radha and if Radha is walking then the shadow falls on Krishna. Boys and girls these days, when they say something good, they don't understand how badly they think about it. And the one who thinks good will leave it and that man will fight with himself all his life. For one thing, if you understand that a boy or a girl loves someone and does not appreciate others, then yes, what do you do? How sad it is to be released after saying yes, He/she will be in trouble for the rest of his/her life, You know that! By what right do you bother him? He/She does not force you to love, You break the heart of a man by passing the time, So let me tell you one thing, if you break someone's heart by playing a love game and passing the time, So you have no right to take true love. You have no right to be attached to it. You want to hurt him/her in the wrong way. If you can't make someone happy, do you have the right to hurt them? Put your hand on your heart and say to someone who has timepassed with someone, do you have the right to love him? Do you have the right to be with him? And when you are asked why you did timepass, So why do you answer MY LIFE MY RULES! I don't care if he/she dies! So you have no right to be in this world. If there is a player in drama, keep going. Every day there are vacancies in the drama company. There will be good employment in the drama company. If you don't understand the language of love, it will work, but if you don't play the move that makes the life of the person in front of hell. Answer me one thing, why did you say that you hate if you have made love? Where there is love there is no hatred, and where there is hatred love is never present.

This is my belief. Your belief can tell me. Thank you.

: HEMILKUMAR P PATEL

LOVE IS TIMEPASS (BROKEN HEART) SEASON 1

LOVE STORY.

HEMILKUMAR P PATEL

ISBN 978-93-5610-384-9
© HEMILKUMAR P PATEL 2022
Published in India 2022 by Pencil

A brand of

One Point Six Technologies Pvt. Ltd.
123, Building J2, Shram Seva Premises,
Wadala Truck Terminal, Wadala (E)
Mumbai 400037, Maharashtra, INDIA
E connect@thepencilapp.com
W www.thepencilapp.com

DISCLAIMER: *The opinions expressed in this book are those of the authors and do not purport to reflect the views of the Publisher.*

CONTENTS

LOVE IS TIMEPASS (BROKEN HEART) SEASON 1

....

LOVE IS TIMEPASS (BROKEN HEART) SEASON 1

(Current situation, May 2020)

A boy named AYUSH. He is sitting in a lonely corner inside the house. He is sitting without any attention. Sweat on his head, red eyes, white shirt, black pants, The body is getting drowsy. Suddenly he started screaming and crying. Endurance is going out of AYUSH's soul. Seems to be haunted by life. So he has another boy, Whose name is Jordan. He tries to calm his down, Embraces, yet can't keep quiet.

What would have happened to this AYUSH, Attach what happened. It became very important to know that.

[Some different situation.

AYUSH goes to the room. The laptop opens And searches, Suicide case of a boy or girl between the ages of fifteen and twenty-five. It doesn't have the perfect figure, Yet 37861 cases came to India in three months, In it, 975 couples have committed suicide, The rest is different girl boy.

AYUSH think in mind."If there is such a period, The rest are killed separately, So he/she may have received love and betrayal. Have some college study tension. This means that even 500 of them have committed suicide due to betrayal in love. And being happy of someone Betrayer, may mean TIMEPASSED.]

PART 1 : Life Introduction

2015

The present times are becoming very difficult. But nowadays, it is very difficult to talk about love at a time when one has to think many times about whether to trust someone or not.

Let's talk one more thing. There is a boy named Ayush. This boy can be said to be very smart in teaching. This AYUSH was a man who used to go to school alone, have breakfast alone and come back home alone, nothing else, he didn't like making friends.Now after passing 12th standard, he has to graduate, so he takes admission in college. Now the householder explains to him that now AYUSH you can't go alone, you have to have a friend who can come to your aid. AYUSH was not even there real situation. What happens now he was nineteen years old, but he had no friends.

Even though AYUSH did not make friends, the way he looked around, it happened to him that even friends are just for the sake of talking. Listening to these words, he did not like to go everywhere. But now it has come to college life that a man who cannot learn in school or at home can get enough knowledge in college to live the life of a man. People learn everything from what they are doing and what decisions to make at what time.But AYUSH thinks one thing, if he comes and goes every day like at school, he will get some knowledge in fact! So he thinks of staying in a hostel. He also thinks that now he will have some fun. He doesn't think that school life was meant to be fun.

AYUSH gets a hostel room in Admissions College, after finishing all the work of Admissions, his family members drop his to the Hostel room. Remember the family, the boy goes to finish college studies or not to suck sugarcane juice. Let's go to the place where the family stays and then go to sleep after the big trip.

This is how his first day of college begins. AYUSH's whole life was going to be a joke, as per future situation.AYUSH did not know what he believed in doing and what happened.Time is of the essence, whether it is good or bad, Even this time AYUSH could not understand or explain to us.Even if the time of the college is gone, if we look at the present, they do not know how the hostel life of the boy and girl is going.But AYUSH was ready from day one to fight in all situations.Let's talk about AYUSH still going to college alone, in the dining hall of the hostel, breakfast in the morning, lunch in the evening, breakfast lunch and dinner was enough.This alone even though other people in the hostel go to the whole circle of friends.he was the only one who kept his attention in front of all the strangers and tried to understand them all. If there is Hostel Life, don't call everyone by their own name but different name. One boy own name Hiren and all called him terrorist.

Hiren came out side and said "Zombie boss."

There the other boy said, his name was Milk Dairy because he was so white. "AYUSH name zombie!"his name was Milk Dairy because he was so white.

Hiren said. "From today, AYUSH's name is Zombie Boss."

"Devil's name is something that comes with a kick movie in a pendrive. It's a waste of water, it's a business. " AYUSH thinks in his mind.

Now the struggle of AYUSH can continue in life but if such a name is mentioned in every hostel, Some people smile when they think of other people's names and take a cricket bat and lend it to me. Now AYUSH goes to enjoy living with an open heart and comes to life U turn.

....

....

PART 2 : Life Struggle Start

College life has now started for AYUSH in which there will be some serious problems on AYUSH and how to fight it will be decided by AYUSH.Going to hostel and college was the same life,Everyone says that this alone cannot survive, Even if AYUSH lives alone without fun,If there is no such work, then it will be lost in thoughts.In the same way, even if time passes in thoughts, this cannot be called time pass.The answer may be something different. Life now begins of AYUSH.

AYUSH understands everything by being alone and tries to understand how everyone's life style is. Why is it different? He fully fined answer. Now a common thing comes out in his life,His arrogance is that even if he commits a scandal, his name will not be mentioned.He also have to believe that AYUSH has the name of doing everything else.Wow really made the antique piece God.

Everyone else in the hostel understands the nonsense and slowly stays together, Slowly changes AYUSH also does not make anyone a friend.The thing is, at such a time, nothing more, the year comes outAnd he becomes junior's senior.AYUSH prefers playing cards and chess.The door to one of Junior's rooms was open, And he was walking out of there,Seeing everyone playing, he wants to play and tries to talk there.

"Brothers, can I come?" AYUSH said.

"Come on, don't ask if you're our senior."One junior said.

"I saw you were just gambling." AYUSH said.

"Are you kidding, not gambling? Mindy was playing." Second junior said.

"Gather ten.Come on, it's not bigger than you say.Leave everything else I am Ayush Patel, The terrorist has been my named Provided, Zombie. My name provided Zombie by terrorist means Hiren. You people have not improved that call AYUSH you can also call Zombie.Now you introduce yourself. "AYUSH said.

"My name parth, this is Jordan,who looks like another parrot is Jill,The second is the Om and the last is the Rutvik. "One junior said.

"My name is Janardhan. But Jordan calls with love. "Jorden said.

"There is no doubt about love!" AYUSH said.

"Don't have fun with the name, just joke." Jorden said.

"Let's share cards. It's all fun."AYUSH said.

Thus Parth leaves the card. And with each passing card, something like this happens.

" Card seen. Friendship is good, second time friendship is also good. Card seen."Parth said.

"Is the name written on the card?"AYUSH speaks looking backcard.

"brother, his girlfriend's name I think."Jorden said.

"A girlfriend, Nice. " AYUSH said.

"Why are you talking like this, brother?"Parth said.

"I am not interested making friendship or girlfriend.I live something like that,I hate girls if I don't have friends,I keep a distance of ten meters.I don't like it at allSuch thingsThe girl who is attached.All is chatter. The girl's name should not be mentioned later." AYUSH said.

"Why hate a girl so much?" Jorden said.

"I don't hate girls, All become blind in this,I hate that.Listen now,

When I was a freshman in collegeAt that time, while trying to understand everything, I came across one thing.The thing is, if this college or any other college has Loving-student moving around.If the recess of college in this hour, I would finish my meal in ten minutes and walk around the college campus and see everything,How many people are walking with their hands on the shoulders of a girl doing Love You Love You,So in the middle of so many people kissing on the hand and looking at the girl in such a way, that this is what I am thinking.I thought I was far from that but at that time I was watching everyone.Then some of the people would sit in the corner and do some weird thing,So some girls set the boy's collar,Boy's collar was not set, what set it to love-ship? Some places student are playing cricket or volleyball.Some no one sees how many of them go into hiding and don't know what they are doing." AYUSH said.

"This called as love but some situation very painful creation of god" Parth said.

"No no, it's situation not created by god. Any painful situation created by only loveship.Attraction is the pull of one another.Mood comes like a washed mouth with fresh spray in the mouth and coloring in front of the girl.This is nothing but Attraction.The language of love is something different that these people do not understand.Boy/Girl commits suicide by making love. If he/she loves, his father/mother doesn't love him/her? 'It was just a saying that if I could give my life for it, I would give my life.'And do love, So why the breakup? Millions make mistakes if they are in love, looking for a good skill out of thousands of flaws.This is not love only for timepass. Etc." AYUSH said.

"You sit and watch a lot."Parth said.

"I am sitting watching and understanding. Betrayal is found in this. Somewhere girls betray a boy and somewhere boys betray a girl. And the whole life of the one who loves is ruined. "AYUSH said.

"Brother, you will fall in love with college too." Parth said.

"I am a writer. Let me tell you a story. "AYUSH said.

"Ohh, that's good. Hear it!."Parth said.

AYUSH said one story.

[TITLE NAME : Love: A misunderstanding or a mistake?

Introduction:There are many things that happen in love, but the way to understand the mistake and misunderstanding between them,That's a big problem.If there is a misunderstanding, let us understand and resolve it,But how can you get rid of the mistake made in it?Mistakes must be made and misunderstandings must be removed. That's will be life. Talk about present situation. The future is simply shown. The fictionalized story depicts emotional relationships.

(Story)

A boy, Who may be twenty-one years of age, On the road situation difficult. Wiping eyes and looking around, he moves forward. Many the vehicles moving are on the road, The wind blows warmly, A new sense of atmosphere is created, And if someone walks down the road like that. Suppose something like this, even in his mind, the betrayal he received this time is annoying. But at such times he needs to have both patience and attention, maybe the thought that came to mind suicide for two seconds, It's very dangers!

But even though the wrong idea has entered his mind, there is no attempt to think well! It climbs the bridge and the river flows under it. The water flowed calmly and he climbed to the edge of the bridge And without thinking, He stepped forward with trying to fall, A man of fifty years, Grab it and pull it off the bridge and the boy's gaze falls on the man. Boy name rohit.

"Rohit, you?" Said the man with surprise.

"Dad, you!" Rohit said in a frightened voice looking in front of his father.

"Did you do this? Nothing is realized! Why did you need to do all this? " Rohit's father Jatin said angrily.

"Dad, I have no idea what happened to me and what I'm doing!" Rohit said in a cried voice.

"You go home and change everything that is going on in your mind if today." Said Jatin, giving peace and he took his by the hand and took his home, where his mother was making a food, cooking and arranging it on the dining table.

"Both have come! Let's wash our hands and feet and come on. " Nidhi said in a slightly funny voice.

"Maybe if I had been a second late today, I would have eaten alone now." If there is problematic situation, Jatin said in a low voice.

"Why, I don't understand!" Nidhi in thought said while talking.

"Today our son Rohit was going to commit suicide." Looking at Rohit's face, jatin said in a slightly sharp voice.

"So! I don't understand anything? "There was a little fear on his face, but Nidhi dared to speak.

"I don't know, you ask." Jatin said.

"What happened, son?" Nidhi asked in a calm voice looking in front of Rohit.

"College, mom." Rohit said in fear, as if his mom and dad were about to say something.

"Girl or something else!" Nidhi said seeing in front of Rohit.

"Betrayed, mom." Rohit said in a dare voice.

"Hey, there's so much talk about suicide!" Nidhi said it was a small thing.

"Mommy, I can't live without her." Rohit said in a weeping voice.

"So, what about committing suicide! That's why I made you big, that's why to we taught you hold finger and walk we taught you! That's why I sent you to study! If you are in trouble, ask us once, how much trouble we will have with your departure! And the girl, who left you, must be in trouble! " Nidhi said angrily.

"Nidhi brought you into this world by tearing your stomach, The feeling was full for you and even if such a thing does not come to your mind, go to your wish, You can do whatever you wants. " Jatin said in a low voice.

"Why go? Not even one percent of what we have endured. " Nidhi cried and said in a loud voice.

"Why, not even one percent, Mom, I don't understand!" Rohit asked in surprise.

"First Nidhi, you calm down, then let it be understood." Jatin said to Nidhi giving consolation.

"If son, your father means Jatin, I have no more hand in this. This is what it is. Now listen to what I have to say. "Speaking of the whole thing, Nidhi said.

(Past)

"Rohit, this would have been 26 years ago. Dark night falls, Lightning strikes, at that time a house which was your father's farm house. At that moment, a girl was shot in the abdomen near the bed in Jatin's room. When the blood is full runing And at that moment his breath was running. Your father then had a gun in his hand. And talked with the girl whose name was Mansi. " Nidhi said talking about the past.

"Mansi, forget about me and forgive me." Jatin said in a low voice.

"Nothing, Jatin, Take care, A mistake occurred, but it cannot be corrected. The next life will be better spent forgetting me. When did you want me to leave you? " Even though Mansi was in pain, she could speak so much.

"All mistakes are forgiven, just come back to my life." Mansi died with so much Jatin speaking.

"Mansi, Mansi." Jatin said in a loud crying voice.

The next thing the police would have found out, there was the police. Tara's father panicked and fired at the police.

(Present situation)

"Dad you?" Rohit said in surprise.

"All situation created very disaster but reality is different. Mansi was special for your father, I am not. Your father loved Mansi so much that he did not love me either. ” Nidhi said in a slightly cold voice.

"So Dad loved Mansi. Love happens once and can't live without it. I can't stay and you, by no means! ” Rohit said in surprise.

"I believe love happens once. But betrayal is not the way to run after it and suicide is not the way to go. Overcame the fear and moved on, Answered her on the mouth, That i can live without you, And I will bring better than you, I will forget you too, Such a thing set in the mind, forget all past and move on angrily for hobby or your life passions." Nidhi said encouraging Rohit.

"It all happens but can't forget past reality!" Rohit asked in a surprised voice.

"Look in front of your father and that he must have forgotten Mansi! If in front of him. " Nidhi looks at Jatin's face and shows an example where Jatin was in a little trouble."Your dad hasn't forgotten yet." Nidhi said in a troubled voice.

"What happened that Mansi was killed by my dad?" Rohit asked the question.

"All situation is different, you show only you eye seen. This was a boundless love. Whether that love was a misunderstanding or a mistake, It was very difficult to identify at the time. " Nidhi said to Rohit.

"Now listen.

(Past)

"It was the first time Jatin had met Mansi for the first time. It so happened that Jatin never looked the girl in the face, at that time, he suddenly hit Mansi while walking. Then all of a sudden his eyes did not move away from her. At that moment, Jatin felt something sweet in his heart. his friends were with his then and they were both watching. At that time, Jatin saw his special friend Mitesh walking in front of him. And gestured in front of Mitesh and Mitesh realized that he started liking her. This is how the first love story started. " Nidhi said talking about the past.

"I'm sorry; I was in a hurry so nothing seen." Mansi said in a hastily gasped voice.

"It doesn't matter, I made a mistake, I didn't see it." Jatin also said his thing.

"Everything is taken, I'm leaving. Thank you for helping me get over it. " Mansi said thanking him for his help.

(Then they both went on their way while Jatin and Mitesh were talking to each other.)

"Brother, you were watching a lot by meditating!" Mitesh said in surprise

"Ohh, for the first time lost in the world of worldliness. I dreamed a lot. " Jatin said a little happily.

"Dreams will come every day now, you will also get the strength to forget us, brother." Mitesh also said a little happily.

"Let's not brainstorm now, you are irritated. I'm going to class." Jatin said gesturing in front of the class. Then Jatin and Mitesh goes to class.

"The one I have been following for the last two months, I will not let you come easily." Mitesh thinking in his mind.

Then Mitesh used to turn around Mansi and when he collided with Mansi in the same way as Jatin hit him from behind, Mansi slapped him.

"What is this all about?" Mansi said angrily.

"Hey, You was coming from here and I didn't see you, so what to slapped!" Surprised, Mitesh said.

"I know you've been following me for the last several days. Now if you think of doing anything like that, I will prove you in jail. Remember. " Mitesh got angry even more than what Mansi said.

"Now, I'll take revenge for the attitude." Mitesh started doing such thoughts in his mind.

Jatin, who was sitting in this side class, did not have any brain in teaching and started thinking differently.

"Let it strike your heart once more,

And again let the head rest on your shoulders,

Try to believe with believing,

Allow your heart to beat if you believe. " Jatin started bringing a lot of thoughts in his mind.

After trying to meet again like this, Jatin and then Mansi also started feeling good about Jatin. The two extended the meeting. The enmity with Mitesh is also growing. What to do! She doesn't know because Jatin fell in love and Mitesh jumped for revenge, In such a dilemma, Mansi forgot whether Mitesh would be really calm! But he does not sit still.

When Jatin was talking to a girl other than Mansi, Mitesh started making a video by studying or editing it. And then he sent the video to his girlfriend Mansi. That video showed it to Jatin, There was something else spoken in it and something like this was heard in the video" I will spend time with Mansi and stay with you and even if I talk with only Mansi, I will always be with you." Then the girl in front said something like that in the video "Yes, if you do that, then I am yours." They both started laughing in the video.

"What is this?" Surprised, Mansi showed the video and asked for an answer.

"Nothing happen, only diverting your mind. Who is planned game? I called this girl to my farm house today. You come and talk. Else, I don't know anything right now. " Jatin said in surprise.

"Is it wrong to show the video with sound?" Mansi asked in a soft voice.

"Hey the video landed from a distance, whether it's a DSLR camera or a mobile, such a clear voice cannot come. You can't understand that much! And so many small and big fights have happened many times and someone is doing it. You have heard such things before. Someone around me is doing this. Let's talk, before that I finished my work and went to the farm house. I will send the address to you. That girl and I will meet you today. " After saying so much, Jatin himself got into an idea and if he knew so much, someone wanted to break it.

Then time passed and when night fell these three met at home.

"This is Rahi, ask her if she leads my project!" Jatin said.

"Everyone will say it well in their own way." So Mansi get the gun and in front of her.

"Hey, this is it, even with a gun!" Jatin said in surprise.

"To be honest, otherwise I would have shot Rahi." Mansi said angrily.

"Oh, the bullet will go off, if it comes out!" Jati said calmingly.

"If you like it, I'll kill myself. Not all of these are everyday choices. The answer is whether you will stay with Rahi or not. " Mansi said with a gun to her stomach.

But it happened that when Jatin's little attention was diverted, Mansi was immediately shot and at that time the gun was fired and Jatin grabbed her.

"Rahi, you can go." Said Jatin as rahi walked out.

Then Jatin sat next to her and started crying, apologizing. What was to happen happened. It was lawyer Nidhi who killed Mansi and hired a lawyer at that time. Nidhi went to meet him in jail.

"It's situation maybe very hard, Also have to understand. I have to listen carefully to your defense. " Nidhi said in a very sweet voice.

"This is not suicide. It's murder." Jatin said with a little anger.

"What! I don't understand. "Such Nidhi said in surprise.

"I did not hear the sound of the bullet. Another point, shot Mansi. So when a Mansi kills herself, she can't throw a gun but throw it in front of me. The gun was a small bullet fired from it; her stomach did tear and hit the back of the box. It's like a big gun, like a sniper's job. " Jatin said in a thinking voice.

"Anyway, Mansi called me before coming to the farm house. I am her sister. " Nidhi said in a troubled voice.

(Present)

"That night my sister told me that if anything happened, I would save Jatin. Obeying my sister, I married Jatin. Before that, what happened? So Mitesh gave the areca nut to kill Mansi. I prove it. I married Jatin. Now you have so much trouble! "After all, Nidhi finally said this.

"No mom, I have nothing to say to you." Rohit said understandingly in time.

"Your father was in trouble but he did not give up. Kept fighting. The second thing is to save if you find a hand holder, whether she loves you. No need to regret if we love, the man who loves us should not go. Everyone in the world spends time together, But another heart we should try to find, All I can say is that someone can leave us, So when we leave it, If she is having trouble then believe that there is love. We don't need to hurt ourselves if her don't love. It's a matter of feeling, son, nothing else. Even a good body will be visible now; Will show big feelings, That's current culture. One thing to remember is that the love you get from your parents is unmatched anywhere else. " Nidhi said calmly.

"Let's, I don't have a problem like yours. I will try to sleep. Now you will keep me away from the girl and save me. I'm sorry if you can. " Rohit said in a troubled voice, clasping his hands and crying.

"Never mind, son, parents are always forgiving. You rest. " Jatin said holding Rohit's hand in a quiet voice.

Then without speaking, Rohit kept going to his room.

Jatin grabbed Nidhi and said that "I fell in love with Mansi, I fell in love, My dear friend Mitesh, Betrayed, Video made, Called Mansi at the farm house, Gun Shot, Miteshbhai had given him a betel nut, You are my lawyer, I was sentenced to three years in prison. Tell me, when did this happen! " In surprise.

"You know, nothing happened. Nothing was said in between. One thing is for sure, I am a lawyer! The story of another spread this rohit, In our name. Whatever it is, he realizes his mistake! Just remember that you don't need anything else. Our Rohit understands the language of life, it is a lot. Think no further. Tomorrow I will tell his something else. All matter solved, you eat. The love between us is the same as before. " Nidhi said happily.

"The thing is, if Nidhi was found after Mansi, then Nidhi would be good. Salute." Jatin said happily. Even though nothing happened, But maybe if it had happened, there would not have been such a big problem. In small talk, rather than leaving the world away from anyone, Good situation accept and move on. Then correcting the mistake or removing the misunderstanding will stop.]

"I have written many such stories, I will keep hearing them for two or three days." AYUSH said.

"Really, well said. Got to know a lot." Jorden said.

Parth jokes about Ayush story. But there was nothing wrong with what AYUSH just said. Parth didn't believe that even something happened that caused her breakup. And he stared at the mirror all night, And he kept asking himself if there was anything in it. One day those who do not believe in God, today a voice come out of their mouth saying God.

(Let's talk about two years later, in between situation talk in season 2.)

Such is the current loveship. Just now times come. AYUSH doesn't even believe in a girl, He started liking someone girl today, It also became a matter of knowing how changed. This AYUSH began to change a lot. For which to be alone in life, He is starting to like someone today and he got lost in the thought of it today. This is the true U-turn of AYUSH's life, which will make AYUSH a better life or bad life, it's not decide current situation.

[Let's find out later in the next part.]

....

Part : 3 AYUSH's love story start.

February 2017

AYUSH started living in someone's thoughts, back he went to be alone, And he went to get to know the girl. AYUSH don't know her name. There will be another man who is going to fall in love in this world. Don't know the facts, steps are taken, That fear is everyone, it's fact for love situation. But this time something different happens. Parth tries to talk to him; Although AYUSH doesn't even talk to anyone.

"Hey, why are you a little lost now?" Parth goes to AYUSH's room and said.

"It was like this before. What's new for me?" AYUSH said.

"Everything is true, But now we feel that we have done something wrong to you." Parth said.

"Nothing like that, just another new old thing!" AYUSH said.

"There's something new and old about Valentine's Day night college functions." Parth said.

"Yes, But it's three day later." AYUSH said.

"Even though it will be three days, we have been asked to decorate the whole college. So the whole college can't be decorated with twenty five people. Many other man need me." Parth said.

"I don't know the girl's name, But all I know is that she is in Parth's class, Let's start our love story on Valentine's Day." AYUSH thinks in his mind.

"Where are you lost? You're not alone, Jill and Rutvik also comes. you take his, I'm leaving. "Parth said.

"Yes, I came ready." AYUSH said.

"I have never talked to a girl and even though I got the time today, it seems like nothing can be done, I'll go to the canteen first and have a drink." AYUSH thinks in his mind.

Papers are recited in Parth class, That is what makes something. Ayush Jill and Rutvik come there.

"What do these ministers do?" AYUSH said.

"Hey, the box is made of cardboard, You go out, the bamboo must have fallen, its spice is to be made, With a hammer and drip to cut three wings in half, Then we will take care of the other one." Parth said.

"So bye bye after work. like this." AYUSH said.

"No, you know, brother, there is a lot of work. Reema, Give me cutter, My cutter is lost." Parth said.

"Yes, I'm going out to cut bamboo cloth later." Reema said.

AYUSH returns and this is the same girl whom Ayush likes a little bit.

"She is sitting alone now. All out at work and this lonely same copy has a habit of being like me. It will be fun now slowly. " AYUSH thinks in his mind.

One minute, one thing seemed to be missing, Parth and all his friends are in the Department of that architecture and AYUSH in the Civil Engineer Department. Then AYUSH thinks back to something.

"The combination is good, architect and civil. I know how to connect everything and why put it somewhere and somehow she will know how to put it. But don't be in a hurry. Do our work now; there is no need to do anything right now. " AYUSH thinks in his mind.

AYUSH goes out and starts working as Parth said. Jill and Rutvik combine bamboo. Many people work with AYUSH. All the boys are talking to the girl and this is the first time and understands their words. Afternoon all member are eat lunch, some of the architect's students a sleep and AYUSH had only one work to complete, next work Wrapping cloth on bamboo. Parth passes by.

"Parth, how can I cut this cloth? Scissors please. " AYUSH said.

"Where did the cutter master go?" Parth said.

"Who?" AYUSH said.

From there Parth looks at Reema coming and said. "Reema, you join AYUSH, He will take a cutter and tear bomboo's clothes and it will work quickly. "

"Don't tear the clothes." AYUSH said.

"Reema understands tearing clothes, wrapping." Parth said.

"Yes, I understand. " Reema said.

It also happened that, Coming Reema Direct near AYUSH, She grabs the finger of AYUSH's left hand with his right hand and pulls it hard.

" It does more than that. There is so much free mind. It doesn't matter to date but Reema broke the record for touch me. That's one of the first girls to touch me. " AYUSH thinks in his mind.

Ohh, love story is start. Is a wonder man, Named Zombie! The feature is the same. In the girl

has gone to see his own thoughts. And then there is the scene where the calm water is deep. Parth now sends AYUSH inside to make a box, at such times Reema is suddenly sitting alone, AYUSH breaks a sweat, Still sitting and working, Then go try to talk, but can't talk. Reema tries to speak.

"Do you like cutting paperboard, AYUSH?" Reema said.

"I'll do it after cutting, how do you know the name?" AYUSH said.

"Who doesn't know you? You're interested in writing a story." Reema said.

"How do you know I'm a writer? " AYUSH said.

"Everyone knows you, the Rector of the Girl Hostel told me this." Reema said.

"Oh yes." AYUSH said.

"Can you tell me a story?" Reema said.

"Yes, yes, why not!" AYUSH said.

AYUSH said. "Listen me one story.

[ONE CHARACTER SAY : Your thoughts will be waiting and these are the thoughts I am going to give to the world. If you don't help I'll do it alone, But in this college and also in other colleges, when someone wakes up and responds verbally to correct the boy, these people will know about a girl and her house. Only then will I be very happy inside, I didn't think much about my house before doing this, I just thought Nirbhaya case,Nine month old girl, Doctor's rap, Then the rap-taking advantage of such a national politics chair, In this, everyone's house cried for the rest of their lives. And with my help, if any house survives, I will do and will continue to do. This is the culture of India I will try to improve till my last breath because the soul of all the raped girls is with me, I don't care if you don't stay. If I start the game, I will finish for them, I will show the world what is wrong and what is true, just change the idea, a lot will change.

A HORRIBLE NIGHT SEASON 1

Part 3.1 : The subject of research

What time is it and what is our society? If no one speaks, then when the time comes, such a person also comes to help. Funny thing is don't know what will happen to people tomorrow then some people become naive then some people become clever. Clever will look good in the job and business, then naive people cheating.

like

It was something like that day,

Quitting can be a compulsion,

But not because of any flaws in the relationship,

Maybe her ears were thirsty or someone,

Quenching the thirst of the ears.

Quenching the thirst of the ears has ruined a lot of relationships, let's try to improve.

23 MARCH 2024

A boy is sleeping in the house and suddenly he has a bad dream, If a Humans in the cemetery is burning, if someone looks strange, if someone sees him walking away in a dream, he immediately screams and comes to his senses,Whose name is Satish,Satish is 28 years old,

His housemaid comes screaming.And this Satish lives in Ahmedabad in Gujarat.Satish goes to the hospital after drinking tea after asking tea from the maid without saying anything.Standing outside the ICU in the hospital, he sees someone through an open glass and tears well up in his eyes.Tears well up in his eyes and he sees some boys coming, so he takes the chocolate out of his bag and gives it to them.

"Eat chocolate, boys and girls." Satish said.

"Thank you." Said one girl.

"Yes, take this speedily. Everyone will get it. " Satish said.

"Uncle, why do you share chocolates?" Said one girl.

"What's your name?" Satish said.

"My name is Rashmita." Rashmita said.

"Rashmita, today is my sister Rahi's birthday." Satish said.

"Where is she? I want to wish her." Rashmita said.

As soon as he said this, Satish's face became sad. It's as if something big is missing or someone is missing.

"She is not in this world." Satish said in a sad voice.

"Sorry. But what happened to Aunty, can you tell me? " Rashmita said.

"Back to the memories! Come on, let me tell you the whole story." Satish said.

(Past 1)

25 February 2020

[Gujarat, this is the city where people come to earn money, There is a journalist who just wants to come to Gujarat and do something new, It is a matter of time.

Tonight,

On such a night, there was a house in a deserted place in Umargam, which connects Maharashtra a little far from Gujarat.There is something to know. A long time ago, someone died or was killed in this house. If a man does not have any news, the journalist thinks that if I bring this news out, it will become my name.But he has no idea about the place.Then it happens that he stays inside the house at night.He looks around a lot as he walks into the house.A little bit goes inside and immediately the door closes, If this happens then it is scary,Yet with courage he slowly goes inside. He hears the sound of glass breaking. Sweat dripped from his forehead. He has a camera in his hand and goes home. Something appears in the camera but no one is in front. Then he sees something that suddenly screams.Then it disappears in such a way that it is eaten by the sky or the ground?How?What night was the ghost?Maybe then the curse is on.Don't know anything.

At the same time, happiness has been looted from Jatin's house.]

Beginning characters

Jayesh: The head of the house,

Jatin: Jayesh's son.

Satish: Jayesh's son has gone to Kolkata to study,

Reshma: Jatin's wife,

Nikhil: Police officer,

Rahi: Jatin's daughter.

(Everyone is sitting quietly at Jatin's house.The family lives in a large palace-like building in Vapi City.His wife is crying,Jatin's father hugs him and sits quietly,Nikhil is sitting in front of Jatin.And his daughter Rahi has been missing for a few days.)

"Nothing will happen now,How long will I look for my daughter,But there is no alternative but to find it. "Jatin said looking in front of his father and police officer Nikhil.

"Hey, after knowing everything, you will get some information about Rahi,We just asked her friend and thought she would get it or that is not found,You have to be patient. "Nikhil explains that Jatin calms down.

"Everything will be fine, son.What happens to our daughter,This can be a little time consuming,The magic is of time, Will be found.What happens to our Rahi,Rahi's nature was to win everyone's heart."Jayesh explains to his daughter-in-law.

At the same time, Jatin gets a call.But Jatin can't speak and then tries to speak.

"Satish's phone has come."Jatin said looking in front of his wife.

"Don't tell her anything."Reshma speaks in a roaring voice.

"Hello," Jatin picked up the phone and spoke.Jatin also had to take care of the grief.

Satish has gone to study in Kolkata.

"Hello, Dad, how are you?"Satish said.

"Just fine son, when will your study be over?"Jatin said.

"Dad called for that.My three month experience will be completed in eight days and then I will come."Satish said happily.

"Yes, come soon,We are all waiting."Jatin said a little loosely.

"Dad,Be prepared for the reception.I will go to college ready now.Just eight days, remember."Satish said happily.

"Yes, son. Let's take care of it."Jatin and Satish both put down the phone after talking so much.

"Comes after eight days."Jatin's words made the whole family tense.

"How do we explain that?"Reshma speaks in a sad voice.

"Hard situation, If he doesn't see Rahi coming now, he will be in trouble.That's right, he will say, why didn't you say first,Why hide it? "Jayesh looked at Jatin andsaid.

"Nothing to say right now,Will know later,Let's just say-He will not stay there."Jatin stands up and speaks.

"It's okay to come after knowing everything."Jayesh said. "Nikhil sir, let's go back to Shimla,And overall, maybe something will be found. "Jatin said looking at Nikhil.

"There's no point in going,The hotel has been cleaned by bringing everything here from there.It has been three months since Rahi disappeared from Shimla.All that is left is the work of the brain."Nikhil said.

"My only daughter,People who went with her today say she disappeared.They say an animal took my daughter.

Where is my daughter today?I had to think a lot for her life.When she came into the world, we all followed him,If she got angry for something after making fun of her, she would bring her up immediately.Now that she was of marriageable age, I kept thinking about everything.I kept thinking about how to prepare.But the question is, where did my daughter stay in the crowd of this world?"Jatin said, suddenly bursts into tears.Jayesh goes to him to calm him down.

"By accepting certain things, Have to move on. I don't know if it disappeared, But what was supposed to happen happened,What an advantage in thinking more now? Jayesh said.

"If Satish comes, he has to be explained, otherwise it will be difficult to save him."Reshma said.

"Leave it all,Don't think too slowly, Jatin,We are trying our best.Now nothing seems to come from Shimla. You have to see a few relationships in college.Let me go now.I'll call if I find anything."Nikhil said.

"Yes, of course."Jatin said.

Thinking that something bad has happened, Jatin drinks alcohol at night and thinks that everything has happened.

It's not hard to get, So losing is not the same thing

It doesn't take long to build a house, it doesn't take long to build a house,

The hospital comes to take all the medicine for every pain,

But losing oneself does not cause great pain.

Let's decorate the house,

So I don't know that nature takes revenge for any mistake, Yes, yes.

....

Part 3.2 : Satish's talk

(Kolkata)

Satish's face is smiling as he puts down the phone.

"Ravi,Come fast."Satish calls Ravi,Who is Satish's servant.

This Ravi's appearance is something like this, he is nine years older than Satish and has a big beard, There are a few cuts on the mouth,One eye is brown, As if something had attacked, But by nature he is good and simple. Then he comes with Satish from the kitchen.

"Yes sir."Ravi looks in front of Satish and said.

"How many times have I told you not to tell me sir?Forget that you are older than me!"Satish said.

"Yes, Satish, was there any work?"Ravisaid.

"Hey sit, I have something to say to you here with me."Satish catches Ravi and speaks while sitting.

"Yes, yes, sit down,You are very happy today brother,What is the reason for this happiness? "Ravi said.

"Hey,I have to finish my studies in eight days.So now I am going home after many year."Satish said happily.

"The best thing to say is,It is best to study in such a way that no time is wasted."Ravi said.

"Hey, a lot of people like me are studying.Living with you, I have learned a lot.You helped me with what I didn't like.We should know whether you were educated or not but you are very intelligent and proud of you my dear friend."Satish said happily.

"It simply came to our notice then.Let's start preparing slowly now,You don't have much time."Ravi said.

"Whether it's time or not, I'm thinking of something special for you."Satish said.

"What's that?"Ravi said.

"I have a party tonight with my friend, Our people are not the whole college.You have to come with me too.DJ has a party with ten or twelve people at the hotel.Enjoy tonight maybe your name? "Satish said.

Night, Satish and Ravi leave to go to the hotel. Once there, songs are played. Satish organizes the whole party, Yet he finally arrives, And a small stage is created he goes on stage and speaks.

"I am Satish,You know you don't play, you don't clap, you don't joke.Let's all get together in the last time to organize this party.After a few days, everyone has one thing in mind, our future is to be created.We will all be under the pressure of this, that is, under the pressure of creating the future.Sometimes if we meet on the road, we will talk, but nothing.I don't want to be upset by all this.I have planned the party for Ravi only. "Satish said.

(Ravi looks at him in amazement)

"Yes, Ravi is just for you.I told you today is a special day for you.It seemed to me that Ravi was a part of my house.We didn't know each other.What happened seven or eight months ago?

(Past 2)

I left home that day to go to college.So my shoes are torn,Went to sew.At that time Ravi was sitting a little away from the college.And I went to him.

'Brother, this shoe is torn. Please fix it.'said.

'Yes, why not!If You Don't Mind,I will take it. Everyone has the right to life as per Article 19 but some peoplecannot see us sitting here.'Ravi said.

(Present, past 1)

Speaking of which, I feel that Ravi is educated.Then I asked everything,It had noneAnd my servant wanted a higher salary.This Ravi was all about housework,So I called her at my house.He would then help with both the housework and my study.If I didn't know, I would learn with him,He knows everything.In my house it felt like someone in this house lived for me.Even if it hurts, he would take careand Ravi helped me all this. I have always considered you as my elder brother. Ravi Brother, I dare to speak today in front of you,Today you listen to me.No one belongs to anyone,I have seen so much in this world,But you continued to help me without committing a single sin.You did not even love money to serve me.You must have thought I was leaving.So you have to do such a job somewhere else.Hey, I'm going home. If I consider you big brother, can't I take you home? "Satishsaid.

"But how can I be at your house?"Ravi said.

"This is my time, You can do a lot of work for me,So it is my duty to give you something,So I call you my big brother and take him along I don't want anything else. Just let me do that, brother."Satish said.

"Yes, brother, that's all there is to it."Ravi said.

("My long running game will now be over by breaking into Satish's house, It will be fun. " Ravi smiled and said in his mind.)

"Let's party now." Satish said.

After Satish, all the friends are having fun together. Ravi also has fun. Also drinks a lot of alcohol, Live as if it were the last day. This is how other days go,Everything is packed. Ravi and Satish then look around the house, lock the house and leave for Gujarat to go to his house.

....

Part 3.3 : Advent of Satish and beginning of Rahi

4 March 2020

Satish comes to his house with Ravi. The doorbell rang. And Satish's mom opens the door.

"Hey Satish."Reshma said happily and Satish will be too.

"Mommy. I missed them so much."Satish comes home talking and Ravi also comes.

"We were remembering.And who is this brother?"Reshma said looking at Ravi.

"Hey, what I said, Ravi does, joins me, this man.He helped me a lot. "Satish said.

"Come on, son, this house is our understanding."Reshma said.

"Yes, the house is very nice."Ravi said.

"How are you, Grandpa and Dad?Everything runs smoothly!"Satish said.

"Yes, yes, everything is fine."When Jatin said in a low voice, Satish became suspicious.

"Why did low voice speak?Is there a problem?Where is Rahi?"Satish saying this, everyone calms down.

"What happened?"Satish said.

"Hey, there's nothing new. If you talk fresh, then it will happen."Jayesh said.

"Where are you hiding something?"Satishsaid sharply.

That's why he sees a few tears in his mother's eyes.

"Dad, tell me the truth, what happened?"Satishsaid,"Rahi rahi, where are you?" Screaming all over the house, no answer.

"Dad, what happened? Do you want to hide it?"Satishsaid.

Ravi also depresses a bit.

"Not Rahi."Jayesh said.

"Where is it?" Satish said.The question has not crossed Satish's mind.

"We don't know." Jatinsaid in a low voice.

"Why don't you know what happened?" Satish said in a slightly sharp voice.

"We don't even know." Jatin said.

"Don't bother me by saying I don't know, please tell me what happened?" Satish said.

"Our Rahi,It was the year of college and suddenly time started playing on his head.Our Rahi was very happyBut all of a sudden, things went awry." Jatin said.

"Tell us what's wrong."When Ravi said like this, everyone started looking in front of him."Hey, if Satish calls me Brother, then I will consider Rahi as Sister."

"Rahi can't wait, Satish. Listen now."Jatin said.

(Then Jatin talks about a year ago.)

(Past 2)

20 March 2019

"Years ago, Rahi was fond of the environment,So she took admission in Environment of Valsad Gujarat.I wanted to give her favorite college and education,Rahi was very happy at that time.Rahi's first day was in college and she went to college.Now if there is a college, there is going to be sisterhood. So she became two special sisterhood, one was Rita and the other was Bansi. They lived together in college.Rita's brother Mahesh took good care of these threeAnd they were all having breakfast in the canteen one day. It is a matter of time."Jatin said of the past.

(Mahesh and three sisterhood are sitting in the canteen, Because of Mahesh's good nature And since there is no sin in the heart, all are together.)

"Rahi, what are you doing, my sisterhood and sister?" Mahesh said.

"Mahesh, don't look back,There are four boys in the back who are constantly looking in front of me.When I come to college from outside, those people are standing on the bike by the door, sitting on it, talking badly and looking badly.Who is it? Rahi said.

"My brother will know he is one year ahead of us. I don't know. " Rita said.

"I do not see the back,I'll see you when I come back with breakfast.Looks so bad? " Mahesh said.

"Oh,He gets up and walks out.Look fast."Rahi said.

"Hey this Ashish and his three men." Looking back, Mahesh said.

"Do you recognize him?" Bansi said.

"Yes, he is older than me." Mahesh said.

"What kind of man is he?" Rita said.

"This Valsad MLA is the son of Suresh Desai.And this college was also built by Suresh Desai.Ashishand three man is terrified of me."Mahesh said.

"Frightened! I don't understand." Rahi said.

"Listen to the former." Mahesh said.

(Past 3)

"In the beginning, there is a party in the college.This Ashish is already doing this because of his father's power.So it's only a matter of time before my college started,Ashish and all his other siblings were teasing the girl.At that time, a girl was being harassed in the middle of college."Mahesh said and explains the story of the past.

"What's my item bomb!" Ashish said.

Jill, Samir, Harsh his friends.

"She is worried,What could be,We're worried too much."Jill said.

("I was standing there listening to everything, And waited for something bad to happen." Mahesh said.)

"Why are you so arrogant?"Samir said.

"Hey, brother, let me show you something, I'm having fun." Ashish said.

"Brothers, if there is nothing between them all, do not do it." Harsh said.

"Hey, you keep quiet, you are scared when you are.There is no need to be afraid of others if you are with me."Ashish said.Immediately Ashish touches the girl's cheek.

"That's what the college owner taught you.The girl looks goodSo bother immediately?"The girl said.

"We are ready, always." Jill said.

"You say go to the hotel,The three of us will be with you,Let's have fun."Samir said.

(Mahesh gets very angry.)

"Hey, come to the hotel,Even if you see our strength.We will be happy too."Ashish said.Near the ear, "or rap."

"I will call the police and let them in,Think of your father, self respect, you are at stake. " The girl said.

"If the police come,So I'll save. I am ready to marry her for two days and then get a divorce. " Ashish said.

"So we are beggars, stay thirsty!We want to have fun too, what can we do?" Samir said.

"Then I will give you a divorce." Ashish said.

From there the girl tries to escape. And Mahesh comes in front of the girl till Ashish goes to catch her.

"Oh, the hero must be ready." Ashish said.

"Which movie did you see, brother?You will be cut at home, brother."Samir said.

"Why did you bring a cutter?" Mahesh said.

"Come on, get out of here." Ashish said.

"You want to come forward with superstition,

The girl wants to run away in fear,

Don't know what's on your face,

But Mahesh Patel wants to wash your face."Mahesh said.

"Speak well, can I win well?" Ashish said.

"Who wins? I want to win."Mahesh looked at the girl and said.

"Ohh, Finally?" Samir said.

"Quiet, Samir, let me talk now.The move reached a win-lose.There are fights in this college, if you are win then girl is yous." Ashish said.

"This girl is nothing object, I just want to save. " Mahesh said.

"Then save." Ashish said.

"I will save her and send her home without harm." Mahesh said.

After all this talk, these people get into fights.Since Mahesh has a slightly stiff body, he falls heavily on these three. Harsh doesn't come in between because he doesn't like it at all.It so happens that Mahesh saves the girl.

"Seen doing this in college,So I will kill you in the middle of college in the same way."After saying this, Mahesh leaves.Mahesh explains all this to Suresh Desai by going to his house.

"Did my son do that?" Suresh Desai said."Yes, uncle, he used to take advantage of his college and harass other people and tease the girl." Mahesh said.

"I'll explain my son." Suresh said.

(Past 2Present 2)

"This is how I have answered it.So you don't have to be scared. " Mahesh said.

"Who's scared? Why were four people watching now? That was to know." Rahi said.

"These people won't do anything until I'm there." Mahesh said.

"But I have something to do." Rahi said.

"Meaning." Rita said.And the other two look at her.

"I mean, I really enjoy correcting people like that,The fun of being with a man after healing is something different.And I will do it. " Rahi said.

"What work do you want to die for?" Bansi said.

"I do not want to die.He looked at me,So he will improve and become like you, Mahesh." Rahi said.

"You speak in your mind, don't you? There will very danger." Rita said.

"I am just fine,I just need your help." Rahi said.

"There is no such help." Rita said.

"No, don't stop." Mahesh grabbed Rita's hand and said.

"But there is a lot of fear and risk involved." Rita said.

"We'll be annoyed." Bansi said.

"Improves,That is important.I have a game that improves." Rahi said.

"Yes,Let me explain later if there is any, I will go now.It's time for class."Mahesh said.

Why did Mahesh get in trouble for talking like this to Rahi? Rahi looks intently and tries to understand. What is on Rahi's mind, no one knows. Is the time good or bad? Time game played, Only time will tell what was wrong and what was right.

....

Part 3.4 : Rahi's love story

From there Mahesh leaves on the pretext of class, This is shocking.

"You know,What are you doing?" Bansi said.

"Absolutely,Did it matter if I talked to this Mahesh about another boy too?Only for this question mark." Rahi said.

"Yes,I felt a little. " Rita said.

"Well,So you just speaks to see this. " Bansi said.

"No,Not just for the sake of speaking.Take sometime, i will revenge,It is a crime to think badly.Four people scared of Mahesh.I will take advantage of it.I just need your help.Trust me i'll be Mahesh's,Don't be like anyone else.The way a little bit loves me,So i love your brother.Play game, Mahesh doesn't know that. He must love me,So much for me.He must have been happy to see me.This will change a lotand I will tell him in due course that I love you too." Rahi said.

"Oh,So you both love each other,But both can't say right now. " Rita said.

"Oh, I can do itbut not now.Just game right now,Don't let him know.This game will awaken Mahesh's love more,If he looks at me, he will learn a lesson.And Ashish and his siblings improved a lot too.Maybe he won't look down on anyone in the future." Rahi said.

"Well, if that's the case." Rita said.

"I do not think so.Also try. If it doesn't get better, it will stay away from us." Rahi said.

"That's right." Bansi said.

"What's on your mind?" Rita said.

"You both tell Mahesh that I want to meet Ashish,And slowly I started to like it." Rahi said.

"You're going to waste of time, I think so. " Rita said.

"Nothing will happen,If you just wait for result. Now you go. I'm going too." Rahi said.

After all this talk, Rita and Bansi leave. Immediately Rahi leaves her bag with a piece of paper on the table, Which Rita sees. Suddenly a boy comes, Whose mouth is covered with a handkerchief, The eyes are fitted with goggles, The hat is worn over the head. He came wearing a black coat, The man sits at the table, holds the letter, reads it.

"Who is this? Something is wrong!"Rita sees all this and thinks. Since the mouth is not visible, Rita falls into superstition and this confusion of Rahi makes me think.

Who reads Rahi's letter? And as soon as he gets out of college.Rita chases after him. But he doesn't get it, runs away.

"What would Rahi have written in the letter?Not now but later I will catch and ask.It doesn't work to deceive my brother.She will play a game with Ashish but he will never play a game with my brother.I'll just hold it.Rahi's game in her way and my superstition in my way.Come on in, take a look and enjoy yourself!Game is start."Rita thinks in her mind.

Then Rita goes to her class, It is thought, So Rahi and Bansi call her.

"What do you think?I'm doing well.I don't think anything bad for Mahesh."Rahi said.

"Yes, yes, I know, you don't think badly.I was feeling a little superstitious inside. Maybe there's nothing wrong with doing good! " Rita said.

"Don't think too much,Rahi also loves Mahesh, it will be good.Don't force your brain to think like this. " Bansi said.

"Yes, just don't think.Now you think. " Rita said.

("The idea is not this Bansi. Rahi hides something big from us. Asking Mahesh to love, he reads the letter again. I'll just find out and jump. " Rita thinks in her mind.)

"Rita,Let me tell you something. In the future I will be someone's, So simply Mahesh." Rahe said.

"Yes, yes, nothing. Let's do our study." Rita said.

("Probably seen my men, Otherwise, I have never seen Rita like this. " Rahi thinks in her mind.)

("Words create magic. I just want to recognize that magic.You are not visible. " Rita thinks in her mind.)

("I do not think so badly. I love Mahesh, The letter taker cannot be brought out right now. I think you're just looking at it and thinking. Time will tell who he is. If I have to release Mahesh for that, I will do it first. " Rahi thinks in his mind.)

"Don't forget to go home or go out of college and tell all game Mahesh to do that much now." Rahi says to Rita.

"Yes, yes, I will say that by going out now." Rita said.

After all this, the class ends in a short time. All are coming out on different routes. Rita Mahesh joins, Rahi separates and Bansi separates. It happens that Rahi is leaving the college, Then Ashish is sitting there all together. Looks bad, And all his siblings are talking.

"It's difficult to talk as far as Mahesh is concerned." Ashish said.

"Only when Mahesh has to do something before he can say no." Samir said.

"Kill Mahesh and make you disappear." Jill said.

"I worked hard a few days ago, You are the one who is fight.Nothing matches the big fight.Ashish gets a clean heart, not lust." Harsh said.

"Don't spoke." Ashish said.

"Brother, keep your mind and pure heart with you.I had heard that one in two or four good men turned out to be a bad one.But this is going to get worse. " Jill said.

"It's not like I'll be with you when the time comes.But you have to have time to do something.Don't hit the line anywhere.She is also someone's daughter, If you ask Mahesh to kill him, he is also someone's son."Harsh said.

"We are also someone's son."Jill said.

"Well, I can see,We'll catch up when we get a chance to do it later.Just wait now.Mahesh and his sister come,So let's go."Sameer sees Mahesh and his sister coming and said.

These people go out in a hurry, Rita tries to tell her brother to do what Rahi has said.

"These people run away when they see,It would have been better." Mahesh said.

"I don't know if it improves or not.I have one thing to say to you. " Rita said.

"Yeah tell me, what happened?" Maheshsaid.

"Nothing happened, but one thing is for sure." Rita said.

"Why is it slow to talk so fast?" Mahesh said.

"Rahi wants to meet Ashish." Rita said.

"What are you talking about!" Mahesh is surprised.

"Yes, she wants to be friends with Ashish, she wants to move on." Rita said.

"But how can she do such a thing?" Mahesh said.

"I do not know.All I have to say is that as long as you live around it she will not be able to find Ashish. " Rita said.

"Why is this Rahi doing this?" Mahesh said.

"She asked to see you tomorrow.You can help her, no one else can,she said." Rita said.

"I'll see her tomorrow alone. Listen to what she has to say.Why are you doing this?" Mahesh said.

He gets out of his car and thinks of driving.

("Rahi wants to do the last thing. Why does Ashish do this even though he knows it is bad? I kept thinking about it and I fell in love with it.It doesn't matter if he says to go with another, but why with Ashish?Rahi does this even though I save it so well. You do not understand at all. Today, for the first time, I got in trouble with you. Maybe you never thought of me, And I never left,So you feel like I have nothing in mind, But you are in my heart and mind and you will be.What do you do for a living and what do you need? I don't think any of this, If this is your happiness then that's fine.

All I have to say is,

Was it necessary to leave?

If you don't like it, why not?

But I needed to understand.

Grief arises,

Not trying to stand up at all,

Sometimes I have to say,

And the time for tears has come.

Would have tried before,

So i'm happy today

But by no means saying,

What does she want without knowing?

Just know today,

And then the sacrifice of my heart is for you,

I don't think so. Now all of a sudden I feel like I've come down." Mahesh thinks in his mind.)

"What do you think, Mahesh?" Rita said.

"I don't think so." Mahesh said.

("Mahesh is in pain but can't say. Rahi also called stone heart, She is doing this even though she knows that my brother will suffer so much. Let me see you tomorrow." Rita thinks in her mind.)

"Truth be told, trouble happens!" Rita said.

"Yes,The problem is getting worse.Why does Rahi do this?She may not know that I have a passion for it.There is a feeling for that. I'm afraid of losing it.Maybe I didn't say it was wrong.I had to tell her.That's my mistake. " Mahesh said.

"Time will tell.But I didn't know a thing."After this, Rita, who had seen a man in the canteen, takes a letter and tells all the answers.

"Someone new came.Now we have to work on having fun.Rahi's telling you this, man with letter, affection for Ashish, it will be a lot of fun to solve this puzzle. Gradually a new man also came.Not a little, but a big scandal.We have to wait and see what Rahi will talk about tomorrow.Just look now, Rahi, you are misleading me.Maybe that's true, I don't even know if I love her." Mahesh said.

....

Part 3.5 : Start Game, wait and watch.

The next day, the four meet in the canteen. (Rahi, Mahesh, Rita, Bansi.)

"Hey, I told him what you said." Rita said.

"Yes, listen to what I was saying, Mahesh.Ashish can't even talk to me as long as you are Mahesh. Then," said Rahi.

"So I say stay away from you?" Mahesh said.

"Listen carefully.This is what has created fear in their minds, because of that fear they just look at me.I want to meet and it looks great. " Rahi said.

Mahesh is sitting in front of his sister as if thinking a little.

"Then something may happen that you go with him,And say that Rahi wants to talk to you. " Rahi said.

"Why are you doing this?" I don't understand anything." Mahesh said.

"The time will come when it will be understood,What more can I ask for now? In the end, everything will be fine. " Rahi said.

("She is waiting answer for me and says everything will be fine." Mahesh thinks in his mind.)

"Where did you suddenly get lost, Mahesh?" Rahi said.

"Oh no, I was just thinking, let me know what you want to do,I can't answer without knowing. " Mahesh said.

"The truth is, I like Ashish a little bit. Then I will be like that.I have to live with someone after we all get college leave from time to time,So I thought so.You explain your way to AshishAnd you says if he tries to talk to me, the girl will never start talking, the boy will have to try.You explain it and talk.What happens next? " Rahi said.

"Everything is thought and spoken, right? Then nothing will happen!" Bansi said.

"Yes, that's right. Nothing should happen then. " Rita said.

"Let nothing happen, have faith.Mahesh, everything will be fine. I have taken action now that I understand who is in trouble. " Rahi said.

"Never mind, I'm going with Ashish.Let me tell you what happened." Mahesh said.

Mahesh leaves and these three talk.

"Rahi, you really take my brother!" Rita said.

"Oh no, I will tell him before the end of six months. I love him.Believe me, don't let Mahesh spoil you.They must have been thinking of doing bad things with as many girls as I did.Looks good, it's not the girl's fault.These people have a bad understanding,Tease these guys just by looking at any girl.When teasing occurs, only one thing runs through the girl's mind ('Maybe if this does something wrong with me, I will not go home, I will not let my parents' honor be harmed.') This is the same thought that confused away at girls every day they come to this college.But what can the girls do who jumps on boy's dad's power at the same time and saves the girl who comes in between these people.But Mahesh has given a strong answer.So I'm willing to sacrifice alone, not for myself but for every girl like me, And history will be with me as proof. The answer is yes, I will tell Ashish and the whole world,No one will get bad idea but if the time given has improved then the world will be waiting for you. Your thoughts will be waiting and these are the thoughts I am going to give to the world. If you don't help I'll do it alone, But in this college and also in other colleges, when someone wakes up and responds verbally to correct the boy, these people will know about a girl and her house. Only then will I be very happy inside, I didn't think much about my house before doing this, I just thought Nirbhaya case,Nine month old girl, Doctor's rap, Then the rap-taking advantage of such a national politics chair, In this, everyone's house cried for the rest of their lives. And with my help, if any house survives, I will do and will continue to do. This is the culture of India I will try to improve till my last breath because the soul of all the raped girls is with me, I don't care if you don't stay. If I start the game, I will finish for them, I will show the world what is wrong and what is true, just change the idea, a lot will change." Rahi said.

"So, Your idea is best, Rahi i proud of you" Bansi said.

"The idea is that I have done well. Nowadays, I am told badly that I am betraying Mahesh.So I do not betray, I betray the bad society.An era of reform is also needed.This will spread as soon as my words happen.It is up to you to help or not to help.I just want an answer from these people to do wrong and this is my right which even the government will not stop me and you will not stop me for your brother.If it goes wrong, the responsibility will be mine and if it goes well, we will all be responsible.If we continue, gradually everyone will join and even if they don't join, there will be no problem. " Rahi said sadly.

"If you have such a good idea, I will hand it over to you, my brother. Whatever you have to do with my brother, I am ready. " Rita said.

"Thank you so much." Rahi said happily.

Mahesh finds Ashish in college till then and he appears in the parking lot. People who don't want to improve look bad on all girls. That is why Ashish and all his other friends get frightened when they see Mahesh walking with them, Ashish and Ashish's friend fear them.

"When will you people improve?" Mahesh said.

"What's your problem,We are fine. " Samir said.

"Whatever it is, Rahi wants to meet you." Mahesh said.Then Ashish is surprised.

"I do not know. What you are say?" Ashish said.

"To be honest,One thing you have to believe is that I will meet you. " Mahesh said.

"Yes, what do you want to believe?" Ashish said.

"Meet Rahi and you too will be like that forever. Rahi is very good. You think badly of the other girls and her but you have to improve and live for her all your life. You have to live with someone for the rest of our lives, so let's live well. " Mahesh said.

"Yes, I will do as you wish and as Rahi wish." Ashish said.

"Yes, I'm leaving now. I'll call and tell you where to meet. Give me the number." Maheshsaid.

Mahesh keeps taking the numberand go outside. Then these people talk inside.

"Why is this happening today?" Ashish said.

"I think something else." Jillsaid.

"Not only you but me too. What could be? " Ashish said.

"Brother, whatever it is, if we get together, we will gradually find out what really happens." Harsh said.

"Don't take revenge!" Ashish said.

"I understand.If you look away, you will know.The first thing is what she wants to doAnd if there is a good thing at all, it can be the same -If a boy crosses the line and the girl sees a little strength in the boy, then he gets fed up.If there is something like that, it will start letting you know in a few days. And we're just passing the time.So something like this passes your time.What's wrong with that, too?If there is nothing to kill, the answer will be found." Harsh said.

"This is the first time you've ever thought of us." Ashish said.

"It simply came to our notice then,The difference is that right now you like what I'm saying.And there is nothing wrong with that.There is nothing better for you than this, and if it is true you will be judged. " Harsh said.

"And if something goes wrong!" Ashishsaid.

"Then you believe me,Whatever happens, maybe something bad happenedSo I will tell you what will be the way for these people to go to heaven. " Harsh said.

"We people are brainwashed into hitting the lines,But then you will think terrible. " Ashish said.

"You brainstorm and your time,Let's try to figure out what this game is all about.

Many would have been kings,

Many will be killed,

There will be a lot of trouble,

So there will be a lot of jokes.

If only they had found a way to make fun of them,That day will be his last days."Speaking like this, Ashish will be a little and immediately looks with an angry look.

So on this side of the canteen, suddenly someone's call rings on Rahi's phone.

"Hey, the phone rang. Let's talk." Rahi picks up the phone and goes out.

Rita immediately wonders who is the one on the phone for which she had to stay and go out, chases and listens on the phone.

"Hey, I wanted to tell you, I'll call you, not you. And how is everything going?But remember that I am with you in case of any problem.I'll call you later when I'm leaving. "

Saying this, she puts down the phone and Rita stands behind her.

"Who was on the phone?" Rita said.

"Oh no, nothing else." Rahi said.

"You were hiding something. Who was the phone call man?" Rita said.

"Ok ok, but don't tell anyone." Rahi said.

Rahi tells Rita that everything will be known in time. (One more story.)

. . . .
. . . .

Part 3.6 : Rahi and Ashish meet

Rahi and Mahesh talk while walking in college.

"I will call Ashish when you say so." Mahesh said.

"Yes, you should, but she should come alone." Rahi said.

"Then you go to the canteen and he will come." Mahesh said.

Rahi goes to the canteen.She is sitting. After a while Ashish is seen coming and he comes and talks to Rahi.

"Can I sit down?" Ashish said.

"Yes, yes, why not, sit here." Rahisaid.

"You told Mahesh something about me!" Ashish said.

"Yes, that's why I called you." Rahi said.

"So what was the point?" Ashish said.

"Something like this is happening,You were looking at me in the canteen that day, I was fascinated by your strength.Then Mahesh would say something before you had a fight,So I thought so you want to talk to me but don't try to come with me because of Mahesh.So I thought I told Mahesh to call you,Let's settle everything and start anew.Such quarrels will never end.I thought something good would happen if we both became friends.Everyone stays together and has fun.It is possible to move forward slowly."Rahi said.

"Next, so I don't understand!" Ashish said.

"Why don't you understand? I have to explain!"Rahi said.

"It was the first time had ever called a girl,So the brain is dizzy,That is why nothing is understood and cannot be understood. " Ashish said.

"All that happen, Talk to you soon and keep up the good content. " Rahi said.

"I didn't ask, what will you take? Tea or coffee?" Ashish said.

"Coffee."Rahi said.

("She asked for it right away without embarrassment." Ashish thinks in his mind.)

"What do you think?" I'm just sitting here. Bring me some coffee. " Rahi said.

"Yes, bring it." Ashish said.

(Then Ashish thinks while having coffee."Problemso don't look.She like a good thing.The rest of the girls are hard to identify.If Rahi is doing something thinking, then she is not thinking anything.But why do I think I have the opportunity to take it." Ashish thinks in his mind.)

Then he goes back to having coffee.In this way, they both get into a talk and Mahesh sees from a distance and gives himself trouble.If by mistake Rahi's eye falls on Mahesh then Mahesh starts running away from there.After talking for a while, the two of them shake hands and go away with their siblings. Rahi meets her people.

"What,How do you feel about that? " Bansi said.

"I felt a strange man. Agar will fall. He thinks a lot." Rahi said.

"Nothing, everything will happen slowly. Mahesh, what do you think? " Rita said.

"It's simply lot happen, Whatever Rahi wants will happen. But you need to be careful. " Mahesh said.

"I don't think so." Rahi said.

On the other hand, Ashish reached with his friends.

"What, how was the first meeting?" Samir said.

"I don't think there's anything wrong with that. Things are the same." Ashish said.

"Then why do you think so much?" Harsh said.

"I things first meeting is very funny completed but confusion high level. It's all about friendship now. " Ashish said.

"So let's talk, if anything happens we're all here." Harsh said.

"Brother, keep your mind on everything, even if we are like Stranger, but your mind should be on." Ashish grabs Harsh's shoulder and speaks.

"You don't take any tension, I'll keep an eye on you, there will be no problem at all, I will keep pointing at you." Harsh said.

"Thank you." Ashish said.

"What did you say?" This is the first time such words have come out of your mouth!" Harsh said.

"I think this girl will be correcting you?" Samir said.

" Why do you have good words for it? We just look at the girl with lustful eyes. We are not going to improve and I do not want to improve. The only answer I can give you is to have fun, I'm not going to get better. " Ashish said.

"But do you remember Mahesh's talk?" Harsh said.

"Now that man is shaking me." Ashish said.

"I do not know. What happens to you is good. It is not good to live with sin in mind. " Harsh said.

"I am just a bad person. Bloodshed, rap, fights make my name shine. I don't know anything else. " Ashish said angrily.

"You didn't think about it when you were in the canteen, why you didn't remember the night, why you didn't want to use her body, why you didn't want to say bad things about her then, or why you were there." Shut up Brother, your brain is used now. Until now, only you thought that everything would go wrong, but today, for the first time, you have gone to meet someone with respect. You are in the mode of change today. You just have to be more discriminating with the help you render toward other people." Harsh said.

"You gave a good speech but I never changed." After saying this, Ashish takes the bike and runs away in anger.

"My brother has a few bites. Gradually, it will get better." Samir said.

"If it improves, never remind him,That's how we all get annoyed. We have to give him time to be alone. If it's good, let it be. " Harsh said. "But what I didn't expect happens." Jill said.

"Times change. If it is beyond comprehension, sometimes life is hectic and sometimes there is an atmosphere of peace. In the meantime, Ashish is completely depressed today. It will be fun, but this time it will be fun to change something." Harsh said.

After a while, that day of college is about to end. So at that time Ashish is sitting outside like a lurker wearing vulgar clothes, at that time Ashish changes from his fun and immediately calms down. Ashish's seems to be coming from opposite Rahi. Then Ashish's brothers understand and go away.

"Is this all gone!" Rahi said.

"Blood is made from bones, bones are not made of blood. If you keep going, there will be some blood in the bones! " Ashish said.

"What you say? Anyway,You don't like sitting in class? You are wandering. " Rahi said.

"Who sits in the class. Let's get through. " Ashish said.

"And what company are these clothes wearing? If someone wears such clothes! Come to a few professionals. You are the son of MLA. Come out of this world for a while. In this way, sitting in the corner, you just get the name recognition and nothing else. You just have to be more discriminating with the help you render toward other people." Rahi said.

"I do not want anything to come. You guys stay educated I'm fine. And yes, I will try to change, please. " Ashish said.

"Change your life style. Many things change nowadays. Think from the heart whether you really are right or do not want to be right. A name will not get you anything, but making a name for yourself will make the world yours. " Rahi said. After saying so much, Ashish gets another answer and runs away.

It's okay to run away, but the next day the whole thing changes. Everyone looks at him as if he had come to a college class for the first time. The whole face also changes. The hair is neatly cut and the clothes come as Rahi said. Then things change slowly. Since Rahi and Mahesh are not together, sometimes Mahesh bring tears from their eyes at home. Seeing Rahi with Ashish, Mahesh gets in trouble but since Mahesh really loves, he stays in Rahi's happiness.

....

Part 3.7 : The fact of Rahi

It's been a while now. Then in a few days his last year's farewell party is planned. He calls Rahi, Mahesh Rita and Bansi in the canteen on the morning of the farewell party.

"Why did you call us all of a sudden?" Rita said.

"The time is up. Ashish has changed completely. " Rahi said.

"Then stay with him." Mahesh said.

"You're angry with me!" Rahi said seeing Mahesh's anger.

"Do you realize how bad that man was?" Mahesh said.

"Everything is conscious and I took that step just thinking." Rahi said.

"No one else came to your notice. He took the name with me and I will try to change it. Then dream of living with him! " Mahesh said.

"You have the right to speak. Then give you a lightning bolt. " Rahi said.

"Why are you a DP's power, you will give me a tweak! You were with Ashish, that's the big tweak for me. What happened to Ashish? " Mahesh said.

"Game over." Rahi said.

Mahesh is completely shocked.

"Game means Ashish! I don't understand?" Mahesh said.

So let the whole thing tell him.

"That means you play with Ashish!" Mahesh said.

"To fix it and It was a small revenge to think badly of me. And it will save a lot." Rahi said.

"You are right." Mahesh said.

"The problem is, he doesn't know it yet, and when it does, you'll be ready to save me." Rahi said.

"Oh, I will save you." Mahesh said.

"One problem is another. Today, he has organized a Shimla picnic for four of us and all four of us. I'm leaving tonight. " Rahi said.

"So what do we do?" Rita said.

"Ok to go. He doesn't know anything yet." Rahi said.

"Come on, let's not let anything happen to me. "Mahesh said.

"So I'm ready to go." Rahi said.

"It's not a problem to go!" Bansi said.

"Yes, but Mahesh I know you love me." Rahi said.

"Yes son." Mahesh said.

"If you want to face someone, be ready, but be afraid to talk. Let me just say, I love you. " Rahi said. Mahesh is ashamed.

"Me too." Mahesh said.

'This is how the two get together which Ashish does not even know. After finishing the farewell party at night, he came home that day and told me everything every day.

(Past 1 present 1)

4 March 2020

Everyone is sitting at home and listening to Jatin.

"I didn't think it was enough that everyone left for Shimla that night, but that night I found out that Mahesh was dead. So it is not known whether these people left Shimla or not. The phone doesn't ring. We were all terrified. A postmortem of Mahesh the next morning revealed that Light Belladonna had been poisoned and that the effects had spread within seven to eight hours. In other words, if Mahesh is killed by giving poison, then Rita will not go for picnic. Then the next day a call came from Shimla that Rahi was not seen in the hotel." Jatin said.

"Then all suspicion goes there, why didn't the police do anything?" Said Satish.

"ML is his son. No police can touch him without proof." Jatin said.

"So Rahi may have been taken to Shimla or drama?" Satish said.

"The house also has bear steps and rahi blood. These people have done something from there. " Jatin said.

"So didn't you call her either Rita or Bansi?" Satish said.

"She didn't call anyone on the way out, nobody knew about it or let her know." Jatin said.

"Can I say something?" Ravi said.

"Did you keep my son safe?" Jatin said.

"Yes, that's right, Dad." Satish said.

"Yes, son of a speak." Jatin said.

"I have three questions in my mind." Ravi said.

"Maybe we can get some answer in your talk. " Jatin said.

"The answer is no,

The question is the first one to which Rahi gave a letter.

Question second : While playing another Rahi game, he hid Mahesh's talk and talked to Ashish, but no one but him knew this? Finally!

Question third: When she go out of the house for picnics, no one calls by name and that is the answer to these questions. Rahi did not leave without calling. Only one call it's proof but they can't. how?" Ravi said.

"Someone called the record not checked." Jatin said.

"You see it, I see what I see." Ravi said.

"Is there any other man among these people?" Jatin said.

"Yes, it's one hundred percent." Ravi said.

"Can there be any way?" Jatin said.

"As you said, if someone has given poison, not seven or eight hours ago. If so many hours ago And at night when Mahesh dead has given poison at three or four o'clock because his dead time nine o'clock something, 3 o'clock the party has started. It's confusion only things 3 o'clock party start then who gave poison mahesh? it's internal peson!" Ravi said. "So let's ask the canteen waiter." Satish said.

"There is no answer. If there is a waiter, then the owner of the canteen also works under Suresh Desai. Suresh will save his son. That is why the man is oppressed. " Ravi said.

"Then the answer will never be found." Satish said.

"The answer will be found, brother. But when we don't show our faces. " Ravi said.

"What do you get for not showing your face?" Jatin said.

"Even the police don't know who we are by not showing their faces. Satish is going to take advantage of this. The two of us will get together and confuse them as they confuse us in the way we keep our game behind them." Ravi said.

"I can't understand." Satish said.

"What's going on in your mind is really strong. Explain to us what you want to do." Jatin said.

"Even if we get these people out, these people will get out on the power of the father MLA. I'm looking forward to it. " Ravi said.

"In this, I have lost my daughter. Let no one else lose." Jatin said.

"No one can be lost. Listen to me done who is in the canteen, who called Rahi, has already poisoned Mahesh as the effect starts after 8 hours of light belladonna poison. These people have meet for a picnic on the way home when he may have fallen ill. And the big thing is that there is no bus or travels and no such train to Shimla in one night."Ravi said.

"You mean, they didn't go to Shimla." Satish said.

"It is also true that those people have not gone to Shimla one hundred percent and Rahi has not gone one hundred percent. What Rahi has done here is still there, but I can't get it." Ravi said.

"It seems to be true, nothing like Shimla can be reached. I didn't even think about it, and it never crossed my mind! " Jatin said.

"No, Heavily planned then work successfully, Someone played a big game. Ashish may know that Mahesh and Rahi will be joining later. Ashish already knows that. Then it may have happened that on the day of going for a picnic, Rahi has been kept somewhere. Rahi is unknown at this time what he will do after leaving the situation." Ravi said.

"If those people didn't get there the next day, then why did they get Rahi's blood the next day?" Satish said.

"Who said they didn't arrive the next day? They must have arrived Shimla the next day." Ravi said.

"Then how can that be?" Jatin said.

"Show them if book a bus or train ticket, or get some travel details?" Ravi said.

"Didn't you notice anything like that?" Jatin said.

Ravi will be slowly smile.

"Why are you smiling?" Satish said.

"These people have also bought the police. Otherwise he checks the ticket first. But he did not take it seriously." Ravi said.

"You mean Nikhil too!" Jatin said.

"Yes, Nikhil, those people have already done what Rahi has to do. If they have already taken a ticket from Surat airport to Delhi as per the plan, it will be four or five hours after going to Delhi." Ravi said.

"Your brain is strong, you will hold on to all the moves." Jatin said.

"I have been winning in the game of chess, the only difference is that this time my vizier is alive and his whole army. I have to grasp each one carefully. Even without fear. These people have kept the magic very strong but I will strike directly at Raja. All will be found without proof and when found, I will kill them by playing like their game. I don't know another thing, if Rahi was telling you everything, then who gave the letter? " Ravi said.

"No, She didn't tell us anything." Jatin said.

"I will hold on to whatever it is." Ravi said.

"Your brain is racing, but we don't think so." Jatin said.

"The reason you don't like that idea is because you kept her grief going, if you get out of that grief you will get an answer. Assuming that I consider Satish a brother and you family too, my mind is still talking about you. I am a player who, with a little brainstorming in the way those people played the game, can tell what happened. This is how I get to the point where they start. Rahi's sacrifice should not be in vain. They also have to answer, that a girl who was ready to fight alone to solve all the problems in college by thinking of everything well, then what happened that Rita Mahesh and Bansi had to go away. The only reason for this is that Ashish has got his own arrogance who has not even thought of a single life to answer him by playing a game with him to think well. Life and life is a word but for me it is different. Life is the whole life and life is the way of life. Life is for someone who dies every day, but life is lived by those who move forward with true hope. The rest is no different. Many have come like this Ashish, if you don't finish my life from scratch, then my name is not Ravi either. I will found all game." Ravi said.

"But somehow you will do all this." Jatin said.

"Reverse situation then action on time.

You must have been sitting on a swinging seat.

There will be a school run in childhood,

Mathematical examples will also be taught,

But she remained trapped in the riddle of life.

A lot has happened or not met,

Not to be outdone, waiting to be answered,

There is a lot to gain but no strength to lose,

Rahi who came with a life of two moments,

I will make your life immortal.

What word should I use for you,

So you have sacrificed for the girl,

The thing is, not even the idea of family,

After that it was a matter of pressure,

Left you what happened,

I also understand the game of the one who bites you.

I was probably someone's brother,

But Rahi, you call me brother,

I'll go to work and finish

The responsibility of that work will be yours, yes it will be yours. But this time, you will be responsible for the destruction of Satan, not for the wrong, and I am ready to be the cause. Yes, I am ready to fight. It will be my responsibility to do justice, and not stop me from doing this. I am not one of you, so no one will doubt me. " Ravi said.

"Are you ready to do so much for us?" Jatin said. "Soon I will bite those people and I will deceive them in the lot game, even without anyone's power. Because wherever Rahi is, her faith and prayers for me will be with me." Ravi said.

"Yes, son, we are with you." Jatin said.

There, Ravi suddenly looks at a photo on a wall.

"Whose photo is this?" Ravi said.

"This is a photo of a swindler living in our house." Jatin said.

"But there is a necklace on the photo." Ravi said.

"I don't know if he is alive or dead, but he is not alive for us. Don't ask about it, son. "Jatin said.

"Yes, nothing. My brain will continue. You go to bed without any tension. It's like a little night. Satish and I should go out for a while. " Ravi said.

"Yes, nothing. My brain will continue. You go to bed without any tension. It's like a little night. Satish and I should go out for a while. " Ravi said.

"Yes, go but don't go too far, it's night time." Jatin said.

"I'm just going to keep Satish calm. He loves Rahi very much, he can't cry. " Ravi said. Then Ravi and Satish go out. Jatin and his other family members talk inside.

"His brain is huge, he is sitting thinking somewhere!" Jayesh said.

"Yes Dad, he spoke hard and I think this Ravi will be looking for a reason." Jatin said.

"Satish has taken care of the lion, now he will roar and attack the other person's house. Today, I feel the last hope. " Reshma said.

"This will not even give anyone time to think and the director will do it again. Everything will have to find a reason. God hears us. He has sent us a man against whom even the best player seems to work. But don't know why this poor man was? " Jatin said.

"Satish used to say that there was orphan in his house, so Satish saved him. After that, if there is such a nature, then we started living in peace." Reshma said.

"It's just a matter of having fun, now we'll find the answer. " Jatin said.

[Satish was in a lot of trouble, what can be done? When Satish himself was broken, someone had to agitate to get rid of the worms of the society. Ravi has come, now the answer was yet to be found.]

....

Part 3.8 : Ravi's talk

What a day it would be, when a brother would say, 'I was not here, and what happened to my Ben in the circle of not being mine.' What would Satish be feeling, what would have happened knowing what happened, what happened to Ben that no one would have even thought of. What kind of people have fallen in the society or this society can be said to be the culprit of those who are jumping on their breath? Maybe today is the magic of life in which people of ordinary family are living under oppression.

Ravi takes Satish out, after night time Ravi starts talking to Satish. But since Satish is in a lot of trouble, he cannot speak. Both of them are sitting at the table with the tea.

"Satish, oy Satish, say something, man." Ravi said.

But Satish looks in front of him and then back at the table.

"Brother, once you trust me, I will do everything as before." Ravi said.

"Like before, will I bring Rahi back?" Satish said. Ravi doesn't say anything.

"She is three years younger than me. I haven't seen her for the last four years. She haven't seen her for four years. I kept it in my heart, it's true that Dad is our Jatin but I saved him a lot. " Satish said.

"Do one thing, you are close to Daman. All the problems will go away and I will be able to sit alone and understand the whole game. " Ravi said.

Then he takes Satish to Daman. Ravi goes to Daman and drinks hard liquor and after the drink is full, Ravi sees tears slowly coming out of Satish's eyes. He holds her hand lightly and then looks at her and speaks.

"Satish, if you have a brother, it is our obligation to move forward even after suffering badly." Ravi said.

"But my family is being punished for something. The only difference is that if we think well of everything, we have to make a full sacrifice!" Satish said angrily.

"Brother, this is not something that is visible. Rahi is not that soon started the game. Rahi is still hiding something. Ashish may have said something about Rahi that we can't talk about. The first and last thing is that if so many people are spoiled, it will not get better in a few days."Ravi said.

"So Ashish pretended to improve?" Satish said.

"Yes, Brightness is the play of improving. All had met his people and he was probably waiting for Rahi to do something wrong. And then Rahi must have known that we don't care Because we will find out only when these people have taken Rahi away from somewhere. "Ravi said.

"You drop my drink." Satish said.

"Take another, but today the matter will be settled and I will start working from tomorrow." Ravi said. "But I still don't understand one thing. If Rahi had said that she would have loved Mahesh, Mahesh would have helped her and taken care of her." Satish said.

"Keep Rahi in a separate place. Rita is Mahesh's sister, if your sister is left, what will she do when she sees you in trouble? " Ravi said.

"Trouble will calm you down after asking." Satish said.

"Rita must have told her brother everything just to calm him down." Ravi said.

"But he was crying at his house, said Rahi to Dad." Satish said.

"Understand one thing carefully, that Rita has told Rahi that Mahesh is crying. So what was Mahesh Rowe doing there? I don't know if she understood. All that is known is that Mahesh cried. I don't think so, and if I think of another point, Rita said it is because he sees both fear and risk. " Ravi said.

"If she had said that, Mahesh would not have turned around, paying attention to him. Whatever it was, Rita would have told him by talking." Satish said.

"Yes, now you slowly understand everything. The second po int may be that Mahesh went to tell Ashish for the first time, He may have said the same thing to Ashish or later, If he gets in trouble, there is no one worse than me. If he meets Ashish, he has said only to improve. There is no problem. That's point noted." Ravi said.

"Why does your brain run in such a predicament?" Satish said.

"It will be a big problem for you in the face of the loss of my whole family, but for me, cut the heart. And a whole broken heart for you. " Ravi said. "I can understand your plight. But first explain to me that you say that if Ashish knows everything then why he doesn't do anything at the same time? " Satish said.

"First you thought, why did Rahi know whatever Ashish was thinking? Uncle said everything that Ashish was thinking at that time. Hey, do you know what is going on in someone's mind? Say? " Ravi said.

"You really think you don't know. How could Rahi know that? " Satish said.

"Ashish used to do this in front of Rahi, explaining to all the brothers and sisters to do it, which makes it seem as if everything we do changes. But he would deliberately show it in front of Rahi so that it seems that Rahi is doing what is right and good. " Ravi said. "Oh, I mean the whole thing is clear. Rahi was playing but another game was being played on it, which is not visible to anyone. And that's what you want to catch. " Satish said.

"I want to capture the whole story. Right now I'm totally unaware, just trying to figure out what's perfect, they're far ahead of us, we just have to overtake and overtake them. It would not have been so easy if Rahi had gone, so the whole thing has to go from the last to the first. It needs to be caught." Ravi said.

"Is there anyone else in this game?" Satish said.

"Yes." Ravi said.

"Dad used to say that Harsh could be so weird?" Satish said.

"Not at all, It is simply brought between a man to leave an illusion in front of us. Harsh is the cause but the game is played by someone else. After using so much brain, What do you think! Harsh may have been shown in front of a character asking to speak simply. The reason is simply that if we sit down to think about everything, there is a man at that point, You can never catch it. That is why it has been deliberately brought out. There is no Harsh. " Ravi said.

"Brother, nothing comes to my mind all day long and whatever came up came going. Now bring another. " Satish said.

"As I continue to talk to you, new ideas will not come to mind and will stop." Ravi said.

"But why do you think I'm depress? What could a similar drinker do? " Satish said.

"Appears in front, Not at all,

Not understandable

There is no living environment,

There is no such thing as an easy night out.

People playing on the field have fun,

Some people are jealous of it, Having fun is just a joke,

Fear is the thing that stays with us while digging.

The talk of love becomes a joke as the days go by,

So no one understands this,

There are so many in this world,

But if the day is good then the man sitting in front is ours.

I don't trust myself because this is the body,

Do not hesitate to betray your own body,

Cancer Blood pressure Diabetes is a lot for the body,

Then such people slowly poison!

The poison that covers the mouth from the front is just a thing of the past for these people,

So what about living in a small situation?

Take special care of the family together,

But what of the outward wrong?

Now for the fun of watching Ramayana Mahabharata,

Did you learn?

Listening to diarrhea,

Got it?

Good talk

What in life?

Talk to someone quietly

But what if we are not calm?

There is so much to gain in this world,

What if there is strength?

There is nothing wrong with that, ask him

Who deceived and martyred his boys,

What if there is no strength from the front?

Annoyingly Libran - always rational, easily hurt emotionally, very passionate and maybe a little too intense.

Talk to you soon and keep up the good content.

No matter how many we are,

Everyone is going to study,

Don't think about what will happen while having fun,

Did everything Rahi,

But not the idea of his compulsion.

Last year in four and three,

Don't think about it in the middle of the year.

It's just that the time has come to fight against time, there is no need to pay, it will only happen when you are with me in my game. I will not come out in the same way Ashish hides someone. In the same way you have to hide me from King. I have to hide to know their whole story. And almost I will see other people too. The wait may not be over. You just have to be more discriminating with the help you render toward other people." Ravi said.

"Everything went really wet." Satish said.

"You don't wear anything, now all I have to do is look." Ravi said.

"Your age seven to ten year, What was eaten! I want to eat." Satish said.

"Leave it all, tell me now that you will be with me in all work?" Ravi said.

"Yes, yes, why not? I am with you everywhere. You are the real man for my house. What you can't do, you have to do. And you have never thought of doing that and the family is not yours, even though all this is my right. " Satish said.

"Now he has kept me. Like brother, I owe you a great debt which was to be paid when the time came and now is the time, To pay favors. If you keep me well, I will give a good answer in return. This will be my biggest battle in the world and you will be my wazeer. 'Let's checkmate' just the two of us. It's too late now. " Ravi said.

What will be the answer for these two people who are looking for a big reason? Will he be able to take the next step? Will the whole situation give way to life? The only thing left to do now is to fully understand and complete a puzzle. To find the man at the center. Both of them have love to find but they are not free without finding it, the rest is about finding Rahi and giving her justice.

....

Part 3.9 : The secret of Ravi

Satish and Ravi have been drinking a lot of alcohol in Daman and talking while sitting there. But when it is time for the hotel to close after midnight, the hotel men try to get them out and they both come out. Then those people the bike ride it but there is no balance. Now in such a problem both of them had to reach home. Those people get out but forget the way, then they take another way instead of coming from Vapi. In a drunken state he cannot know the way. It also happens that instead of Vapi, another road is taken, so the road to Umargam is taken. Leaving Daman, he takes the road to Hanuman Dada Kalgam temple of Nargol and reaches Umargam from the back road. When these two ghosts from Umargam arrive at the side of the house, it is half past twelve in the night, the bike stops at the same side of the house.

"Leave it now, bike off." Ravi said.

"Nothing. I'm going to sleep on a bench here. We'll leave in the morning. Let's go to bed here now. " Satish said.

"Brother, you are so tight, I have to find a way." Ravi said.

Then Ravi's eye falls on the ghost house.

"This house doesn't look closed, it would be nice to get something from this house. Let's go to this house, Satish. If we find something, it is good. We will get a place to sleep. " Ravi said.

"Yes, let's go then." Satish said.

Then a man comes to some distance outside the house and he sees these two people going into the house.

"Brothers, don't go into that house, that house is made of curses. All its walls are cursed. Stay away from that house. The ghost spirit lives in that house. You can't come out if you go home. Your body will be found in the morning. " The man said.

"My Sister is not in this world, we are about to die right now. We are going to die. What else?" Satish speaks while he is drunk, ignoring the man's words.

"Should I go in?" Ravi said.

Then the two of them open the answer door inside. The door closes like a few go inside.

"Hey, this is what happened, Ravi Bhai, get out, open this." Satish said while trying to open the door.

"It won't open now, let's go home." Ravi said.

There comes a flying stick from behind Ravi which Satish sees.

"Come down Ravi, the stick has come." Satish said with complete panic.

"This house, That is what must have happened. It seems to me that I must have come here someday." Ravi said.

"How did you come to Gujarat when you first saw it? But my whole being is torn this time. " Satish said.

Then it happens that if these two are standing, then Jummar falls from above, then both fall against each other. So there is a glass attack on Ravini. So Satish is attacked by some bricks. If it beats a little, it screams where it falls. Both of them have something on their head and feet. Both are in great pain. Even so, owning one is still beyond the reach of the average person. Ravi sees some things that get stuck But from there, Ravi suddenly disappears and starts running in panic, So he doesn't know that there is a whole glass plate in front of him which is visible through, So by mistake it hits him and it hurts him a lot. So all of a sudden he sees a girl and tries to go after her. At that moment Satish gets up and sees a ladder in front of her. So the Ravi appears above but it is not the one whose appearance is different, it looks bloody, So he thinks that if something happens to Ravi, he screams and leaves, but arrives like a bad situation. Takes on a monstrous form of ghost, Seeing him, he immediately run in the opposite direction and ghosts started appearing everywhere. So he runs to a room. Where Ravi has already reached and he has written a lot on the wall of the room and on the loose papers. Ravi can't recognize the letter on the wall but the papers in his hand show Satish.

"Let's see, Rahi has written." Ravi said.

"Ravi, why do you know that this letter belongs to Rahi, who are you, who knows Rahi in any way, You has never come to Gujarat, then you has not even seen Rahi and can recognize writing Rahi in any way, why you does not speak." Satish said.

[Who is Ravi telling everything to Satish?]

(Past 2)

Remember the letter? I am the man who took the letter to the canteen. I am the only one who can take off the clothes and the hat. Taking a note that day, I opened my mouth for a moment. And that face was seen by Rita. I felt I immediately hid my face. But when my phone rang over Rahi, Rita told her who the man was and Rahi told Rita everything.

(Past 1 present 1)

"Who are you? Why should Rahi give you that letter?" Satish said.

"Did he see the photo in your house that I said was the necklace?" Ravi said.

"That is my deceiver brother Hemil's. But what do you have to do with it? " Satish said.

Then what Ravi has slapped on his mouth is not slapped, The face looks different so it has a sticker on it. It removes the sticker, removes everything that is attached to the mouth.

"Hemil you!" Satish said in full anger.

"Yes, Hemil." Hemil said.

"You lived in my house and did not let us know. You stayed in our house and dug back." Speaking so angrily, Satish grabs his collar.

After doing so, he starts beating Satish Hemil. Hemil eats a little bit, but there is an older brother, both of them are hitting each other and both of them are talking while hitting each other.

"You came back after separating my house. If this happens to my sister with you, then it is sin for my house." Satish said while beating.

"Satish, I am not a sin, the truth is not what you see from the people. I was slandered, and you believed the words of those who came to slander me. " Hemil said hitting Satish.

" Don't be ashamed to say this with your mouth! You did such a bad job, so fired you. " Satish s said.

"If my work was wrong, why would Rahi be with me? I have been imprisoned for seven years. While in prison, I made all the plans to come to this house and decide what happened after listening to me. " Hemil catches Satish so that he can't let go and leaves him after talking so much.

"After all this, how can I trust you?" Satish said.

"Rahi trusted by me. For me, that is no longer my sister. So someone has to believe. Once you listen to me, think about why Rahi was helping me? " Hemil said.

"Rahi can understand you, so what happened to you?" Satish said. Hemil laughs a little and speaks of the past.

(Past 2)

Nineteen years ago today. We were residents of Gujarat before. Dad got a job in construction in Kolkata. Then gradually got a job, collected money and became a builder myself. Maybe it was about a time when I was very young, old enough to play. When you were born, I named you Satish. And I was nine years older than you. When I was young, my life was spent in fun. Then the house we were in till now is buy from Kolkata. At that time there were some middle class people living in our neighborhood. When we were little, we used to have a lot of games with our neighbor's son Sahil in the field of our house. So a lot of boys playing and waking up and having fun is about the day when you come and go but go to sleep, so I would invite everyone to play at home, and even mom and dad would be happy. Not even stopping. That day we would wake up in small talk and stay together.

"It's my turn." Hemil said.

"If he's move is gone then my comes, Then if you forgot, it came back And who will come after you because of your mistake? " Sahil said.

"Hey, hey!" Hemil said.

"If only you had spoken." Sahil said.

"Oh no, you are making it by mistake. " Hemil said.

That's why we used to wake up and Dad would come and explain to us and we would start playing together again. If not now the case of life is understandable. As the days went by like this, I was also very strong in teaching. Sahil and I read together at night and get up the next morning to go to school. Then we will grow up. We grew up and Dad would explain to me a lot about what's going on in the world. It was fun living life. It is happening everywhere. Sahil and I were more brothers than friends. When you were twelve years old then I was twenty one years old, my father made me a civil engineer keeping in mind to save his business and Sahil also became a civil engineer. Then Sahil's condition was a little less so I told Dad and took him with me. We sat together and had fun in my well-paid office. Now Rahi was two years younger than Tara. We all lived with a joint family in Kolkata. Now the time has come for us. Sahil and I and our family thought that we should go to Kolkata and live all day together. Took a look. One day Sahil and I were sitting in the office.

"The government officer is coming to check the details and materials of our bridge, you go there. " Hemil said.

"I'm not going anywhere. You go. I won't go in such heat." Sahil said.

"Hey, You have to go. I'm going to pay bill for the tender for the new bridge." Hemil said.

"Hey, I'm kidding, I'm leaving." Sahil said.

Then he goes out and I will pay the tender bill on goverment office. I left the office. There was a call that the bridge had collapsed and Sahil came under it and Dead. At that time I didn't know what to do. Our group was salvaged from all sides. Didn't know where to go or what to do? On one side Sahil died and on the other side my built bridge went. There was no problem with the bridge collapsing. I dropped everything and went there. Sahil was not known. Tears welled up in my eyes. Then goverment went for material testing and then found that the steel bonding used with C grade cement lime did not hold like OPC cement and the steel used used higher carbon steel instead of using thermal TMT bar which did not lift the weight of the bridge and caused the bridge to collapse.

Then Dad alone checked the material written in his report and it happened that he wrote everything differently from the tender we had put, so I felt that someone was deliberately crime us. Then Dad's warrant came out. Dad was arrested. Then I took the material myself and checked the bridge in our lab. When everything was fine, I felt that someone had done everything with the whole plan. Deliberately also changed the material and papers from the office. When they were taken to court for the first time, they checked the material face to face and after doing anything, they gave a week's time after opposite winning. I kept trying to find everything. I didn't get anything then the thing was that when our business was far ahead a Priyank Mistry was a builder because of us he could not get tender and he had big hands on his head. After Daddy was brought in a fortnight later, I did not see any solution, but I stood up while the judge was punishing Daddy.

"Sir, I want to say something." I stood up and said.

"Yes, come here and talk." The judge said.

"Thank you for putting my case in court." Hemil said.

"Yes, what were you saying?" The judge said.

"After changing the papers from the office, I asked the artisan to apply duplicate material. Dad is not to blame. I thought from which godown the material would be cheaper to bring and the remaining money was to be kept for another bridge so that I could make another tender in my name." Hemil said.

"So you take the responsibility of changing the paper and material?" The judge said.

"I take full responsibility. It is my fault that Sahil is dead. I did it for money and it happened to me. In a few days everything will be fine but I did not know that Sahil dead. " Hemil said.

After that I was punished for fourteen years in Kolkata so India time is seven years. Dad even slapped me. Then they decided to come to Gujarat.

(Past 1 present 1)

I finally came to see Rahi that day. I cried a lot because he was coming to Gujarat. I would play it in my lap and make him big. He was confident that I could not do that. All the other opponents in the house were there, but my father never looked back in front of me. For seven years I was in trouble. Rahi informs me in another way where we are. Taking a selfie on Facebook and posting a photo in a way that shows the space behind. Then he gave me a letter and told me heart bit was written in it.

She wrote in the letter, "How are you Hemil bro. I've been waiting for seven years and I thought you'd come out and try to find me first. But a very good effort is to find me on Facebook after your Dirac came here first. I also thought that if put a hint somewhere, you will understand. Jail is a very bad place but I don't want to go there without any bends. But nothing in the whole world can understand you except me. Leave it at that, let's talk now. Satish lives in a house in Kolkata and his servant is gone in a few days. Satish needs a servant. Do it as soon as you can and yes I will wait for you. I love you Big Brother. "

"Just think, no one but me and Rahi knew what I was going to do. Rahi has helped me a lot. So Rahi was my world. You have all the family members attached to you but my family was empty enough till now. I had no one else. Alas, when I heard that this happened to Rahi, I was in more pain than you. My sister One who was with me was also gone. I'm sorry to hear that nature is taking revenge. I was robbed of everything attached to it. Was it necessary to remove sister? The problem is with me the most. My fur was high but who should I tell?

If the way of life changes, sometimes life is shortened,

If not here's a new product just for you!

I thought I was too big, but looking back no one thought,

There is no one like me in this world, so she also separated and went away.

I lived my life with understanding, then someone misunderstood that understanding,

I sacrificed, I did not see what would happen,

In search of who I am, who is laughing at our trouble,

If anyone was found, he would immediately walk away from me.

If I suffer from my own mistake,

Which has no end?

If the end is the same for me,

When I forget everything, when I am one of you.

Farewell to my time,

What I thought was good,

Don't like so much,

With the idea of who is with,

But now i have to live just to give justice. Then I will go far away from you. Just help find the truth. " Hemil said.

"If Rahi thinks this way, then you are right. All I know is that Rahi will be with you. Hemilbro, I will stay with you and help you find out everything. If you are telling the truth, then the truth will come out." Satish said.

"Before that, we have to find out what happened to Rahi. This is enough evidence to give him justice. First we have to look at what happens next, let's talk about what to do first." Hemil said.

"Yes, that's right." Satish said.

"Thank you for listening to me." Hemil said.

"Right now, there is nothing but listening to you without proof. Let's get this over with first. " Satish said.

....

Part 3.10 : Rahi's mysterious story.

After both Hemil and Satish have finished talking, he looks in front of the wall where the letter is written anyway.

"This wall can be read, at first I think it is rough." Hemil said.

"Didn't you write the address number in the papers?" Satish said.

"That's the decent thing to do, and it should end there." Hemil said.

Then they both sort the cards by number.

"Now what is read writing?" Satish said.

Then Hemil takes refuge while watching and Satish gets frightened.

"What happened, brother? Why do you look like this?" Satish said.

"The man at the center was found." Hemil said.

"Who is it, say brother?" Satish said.

(Past:2)

Hemil understands Rahi's whole thing and tells Satish.

Throughout this story, when Rahi started the game, she used to say that if Ashish looks bad in front of me, then I will do everything badly for him.

When she was about to go for a picnic, Rahi left the house and Harsh put her in the car and brought her out of the house. It is like a forest behind her, there is fear. At that time, except for Ashish Harsh Jill and Sameer, there was another man whose whole brain was there.

(Past 1 present 1)

"Did Bansi stay at the center and do everything?" Satish said.

"Yes Satish." Hemil said.

"How about that?" Satish said.

(Past 2)

When Ashish saw Rahi in the canteen for the first time, he got up and started walking. Bansi must have gestured. She had already told Ashish about the game to be played after that. After that, Ashish started showing exactly what Rahi wanted. Then he did something that made Rahi feel that Ashish had improved. Later, when Rahi told Mahesh everything, he got it from the poisoned Bansi of Belladio in coffee. Taking out the excuse of picnic, Bansi called Rahi out of the house. Harsh then took her and came here to this house. It was twelve o'clock at night when people other than Harsh got together and raped Rahi, then To take her blood and closed the house from all places. Rahi then committed suicide by writing this.

(Past 1 present 1)

"It means Rahi lives in this house as a soul!" Satish said.

"Yes." Hemil said.

"Then why did Rahi attack us? He did something that would kill me. " Satish said.

"Where did you hit that talk?" Hemil said.

"If so, where did it disappear? All of a sudden, the bleeding stopped! " Satish said.

"She gave us a way to get to this room." Hemil said.

"But we are her brothers, was it necessary to kill?" Satish said.

"No, The plan was to bring us here by giving us the way we were going. And I don't know if there is anything else written on the back, but I will definitely find something else. " Hemil said.

"So you haven't got the whole thing yet?" Satish said.

" As I was approaching, I saw a camera lying down and I saw some recording in it. There was a girl who used to come and cry every day and then she said that I will kill anyone who sets foot in this house. I will kill all who are in the shadow of this house in my fire, The ghost is known a bit so I thought of going after it. After I got this room, there is still a message that goes out of my mind. She was talking about killing everyone, but why did we both survive? " Hemil said.

"Maybe you know we're brothers?" Satish said.

"It could be." Hemil said.

Then something is written on the wall. And it seems to them that Rahi writes but also writes.

Rahi said "I know my dear brother Hemil is here. Brother Hemil, you are my last hope. I have given up, now you have to see. Let me just bring these four and Bansi five to this house. Thank you brother.

"It will happen. What was left in our love, sister, I have never thought that you and I have made a mistake, I have not forgiven. I twas the eldest of the siblings. I would have done it and I would have stood in front of you. I would never have let Ashish's plan succeed. She didn't tell me this, so I had to suffer the consequences. In the last breath of Mahesh and yours life, I will take revenge as powerful as the wail that came out of my mouth. Your brother Hemil gives this testimony. I promise I will bring them all here before you soon. This night is not for ghosts, but for my sister revenge time night" said Hemil angrily.

"My sister's killers should not be spared." Satish said with tears in his eyes.

"Don't cry Satish, this is not the time to cry. Now is the time to fight war. It's time to attack face to face. Don't give a tear in the eye if you want to give a hard fight. I have raised Rahi in this hand. I taught her to walk, I taught her to live in the world, I fed her with my own hands and raised her. So the thought must have filled me with anger and love for it. This is not the time to cry.

In this fact of time,

Not to be outdone when it comes to war,

You have to fight, if not this way, then another way,

But don't get loose without a fight.

What situation was waiting!

If I had to kill,

The way you hate yourself in life,

So the brothers will get the answer too, "said Hemil angrily.

(The whole thing happened in the same darkness as the house on Road.) : Season 1 completed.

]

"What happened next?" Reema said.

"Will we finish everything today? There is still a lot of time, then I will say." AYUSH said.

"Never mind. You write really well." Reema said.

"Thank you." AYUSH said.

"The Rector of Boy Hostel doesn't know I'm a writer, So how does the Rector of Girl Hostel know? No one says this except Parth, That means Parth has made a proclamation. And this is something I don't know. Now speaking for the first time. Nothing should go wrong." AYUSH thinks in his mind.

AYUSH returns to the hostel. In this way the days went by at work and slowly talking. The Valentine's Day function also came to settle. There is no way to talk now, AYUSH thought let's talk to Ankit Joshi, the rector of Direct Hostel. AYUSH went to Ankit's room and started talking.

"Why Ayush, what do you need?" Ankit said.

"Tell me the truth about who I am. " AYUSH said.

"Everything is fine but don't mix your thought another people, You will learn to mix and match thought." Ankit said.

"I want to mix but add a girl." AYUSH said.

"Oh well, when did that happen?"

AYUSH does the whole thing talk.

"If that's the case, talk now." Ankit said.

"Nothing happens without Parth's support, Listen to what I have to say. Now in the month of March the prestige of the college temple is to be keep, Such a thing has been found. Until then I will do nothing. Then the whole hostel boy/girl is to be put to work because it's a holiday in college. The two hostels boy/girl will work together. Parth should be with us, when some boys going hotel after function. And you forcing me, it's type of ragging, after sometime Reema name out of my mouth, it's situation is maintain that's night. Can you do that? " AYUSH said.

"Ohh, ragging. Why would you want to do that? " Ankit said.

"By ragging, The name will be taken, So the lamb appears, In the presence of all, And people will think it's naive. If he fell in love with someone, he would be doing too much and yes, All will think so. I just fell in love. If something good happens, trust me, I will save it for the rest of my life. She will never be betrayed by me. " AYUSH said.

"You don't even think of betraying, We know you. But if you look at the naive, the respect will increase, Your brain is used, very interesting. " Ankit said.

"I am a writer, so I would write a story." AYUSH said.

"That is why he lives alone, Something is written in the quiet sitting garden. Now comes the U-turn that will change you. But give me some faith. " Ankit said.

"Yes!" AYUSH said.

"Something bad will happen in the future, You might be betrayed, So no day breaks and life you does not give up. " Ankit said.

"Say something good. "AYUSH said.

"AYUSH, you have been here for two years, I have been for the last eight years. I've seen a lot every day in college, and you have won the hearts of almost everyone. Makes you first in everyone's fun. Someone goes playing yours soul and you get in trouble, Please don't give up. " Ankit said.

"Fact, I will not lose. And If anyone will play, So I'll do the checkmate." AYUSH said.

"And you have support." Ankit said.

"I'll be right back. Otherwise, other people will start thinking of something. "AYUSH said.

"Ok." Ankit said.

Ankit thinks in his mind," Life of AYUSH is good happens, Any problem don't come. He is such a cool man, if someone breaks his heart, he can't bear it. I think AYUSH will not be give up. I will save it. "

AYUSH thinks of going out of the room. "Let's get the rector's support. No one can stop me on campus now."

Just then the days go by and the day of prestige comes.

(Future situation)

AYUSH stands on the tracks of railway train. The train in front appears to be coming. It is learned that he is going to commit suicide.

....

Part 4 : Ankit and AYUSH both planning

Now came the day of the prestige of the temple. There was nothing wrong with going the way AYUSH thought. But Ankit's mind was not calm. Looking at AYUSH's face, he pity was coming and AYUSH used to say in a gesture that nothing will happen to me, Think not so much. Now after dinner at night at the request of AYUSH, many hostel students are gathered, Seven or eight people are sitting and talking.

"AYUSH, you are going to be an architect a lot from now on!" Ankit said.

"Nothing, brother." AYUSH said.

"Speak, if so, what is the tension?" Parth said.

"No, no, nothing else." AYUSH said.

"Brother, if anything should not go out." Ankit said.

"Ok, no problem." Parth said.

After a while

"Reema, Reema Patel." AYUSH said.

"Ohh, khemi!" Parth said.

"Hey ..... No khemi, reema." AYUSH said.

"Hey, reema's named Provided." Parth said.

"Ohh, Another name not found, that name khemi provid!" AYUSH said.

"Both are the same, Khemi Zombie." Parth said.

"Both are the same, so I'll talk." AYUSH said.

"Come on, my support in setting the love story." Parth said.

"Ours too." Jill said.

"You don't stay in the side between the rays, the stakes will be decided." Parth said.

"I just said, good create situation." Jill said.

"Let's talk about reema now." Parth said.

Then these two or three people have gone to the hostel on foot, So all of a sudden Parth Direct calls Reema.

"Hey, it's need help to me." Parth said.

"Yes!" Reema said.

"Hey, I have a friend, He want to be friends with you." Parth said.

"Who?" Reema said.

"His name is AYUSH, Talk to you soon and keep up the good contact." Parth said.

"I have to think." Reema said.

"Yes, You would think so." Parth said.

"I'll talk to you later." Reema said. Then the phone talk hangs up.

"She takes time to think, to give." Parth said.

"If you don't mind, but the whole history tells me. " AYUSH said.

"Whose?" Parth said.

"Reema." AYUSH said.

"Ok, no problem. For now, Facebook request can send." Parth said.

"Yes, let's do that." AYUSH said.

"Just slowly, don't speedily work." Parth said.

"Yes, it does not matter. Somehow you can tell me the whole history, somehow get it? " AYUSH said.

"It will be found, I proposed to Divya and answer is yes. then divya and Reema both are friend." Parth said.

"I used to send Facebook requests while talking. " AYUSH said.

"We too." Jill and Rutvik both said.

"What, Who told you?" AYUSH said.

"Nothing, we don't talk, you do." Jill said.

"Like the Rodies game, Now i have to talk. A fear in everything. But I will use this fear to build my strength. " AYUSH said.

"friend, if we believe in friendship from the heart, That is to say, if anything goes upside down, you will not lose Patience. " Jill said.

"Don't come that day. I will not lose but even broken." AYUSH said.

(Future situation Poem.)

The time has come,

Did not understand ,

There was no saying in the talk,

Love is born from the heart,

Can't wait to break it,

I thought a lot came together in my mind,

Meet with friends at that time,

I'm afraid I'll be betrayed by friends,

But this mirror was found,

What is said on the mouth,

I meet friends, who understood my feelings,

The time has come for me to Wounded,

I meet the friends like broken heart.

(Present)

"Let's some work, I have to ask Ankit why did you say this in the middle of all? " AYUSH said.

"Ok, Don't worry." Parth said.

AYUSH then goes to Ankit's room.

"What happened?" Ankit said.

"Yes, a lot has happened but one problem I had to tell you. Parth can't be trusted person."

"Why?" Ankit said.

"Because you want to know a man, So you have to ask the people living next to him. I asked a lot of real people from his college and that was the answer, Seeing that girl makes him loose and Shows arrogance. There he goes to keep himself high profile. If he helped to set up, I would probably have to save themselves

From Parth." AYUSH said.

"But he seems like a simple man." Ankit said.

"But now the people of the college cannot be overlooked. I'm going to my room right now, I left a message on Facebook. Now it is set in some way." AYUSH said.

"Yes, it does not matter but any have problem! Call me." Ankit said.

A few days go by, this is how things go, Ayush and Reema both people's. AYUSH talks to other friends in college, AYUSH gets a lot of stories about Parth. Parth does not know this at all. But Parth goes to AYUSH's room with an information about Reema.

"Reema's got one stories in her past." Parth said.

"Yes, talk." AYUSH said.

"She has a best friend named Divyesh." Parth said.

"What's the tension with a best friend?" AYUSH said.

"Loveship is always start the best friend." Parth said.

"How long has it been?" AYUSH said in amazement

"Three or four years, she says." Parth said.

"Then will be no tension. I talk about something but she don't talk about it personally. " AYUSH said.

"Maybe she doesn't want to talk to you or move on!" Parth said.

"Don't think too much, I proposed her today, Talked a lot, Feeling for you But do not believe." AYUSH said.

"Don't do that, no speedily move on." Parth said.

"Was not going to happen, Let's just talk. What you told me before if I win Dhruvi's heart, then Rima's heart will win. I'm good at Dhruvi's mind, That your college friends Tejas and Kishan Pandya, He told me that I was fine impression dhruvi's brain. We have been talking for three months but no response has come yet. So I'm ready to go my own way and that's my way. I want to see her happy, The other thing is I have true love. Trouble happens to me right now, but first someone took a promise from me That I will never give up and never lose." AYUSH said.

"Did you do it on purpose? " Parth said.

"Now I will see her happy and I will be happy." AYUSH said.

But now God had written something different in the horoscope of AYUSH. Reema's name was spoken in the middle of it all, So all student is to do annoying, What happened now annoyed Reema a lot. So her friend calls AYUSH in the college canteen the next day. And there will be AYUSH's insult.

....

Part 5 : AYUSH's Insult

AYUSH has spoken a lot to strangers, The force to love is also done. It very trouble situation. The next day Dhruvi called him.

"Hi AYUSH, I speak dhruvi." Dhruvi said.

"yes." AYUSH said.

"Can you come to the canteen?" Dhruvi said.

"Yes, that's right now." AYUSH said.

Then Did call disconnect by dhruvi.

"What to talk about in the canteen? Who to ask? Don't ask Parth, He met me along the way. Sandeep was in college. Right." AYUSH thinks in his mind. Sandeep is in college and the call comes from AYUSH,

"Yes, brother." Sandeep said.

"Dhruvi's phone To come, what's the matter? " AYUSH said.

"It's situation is very dangerous, But I said if you have something to talk about, call an architect, not canteen. But no one believed. There is a plan to bring down your dignity. " Sandeep said.

"Not at all, Because my identity is simple man. "AYUSH said.

"Whatever happens, Understand there and make a decision. " Sandeep said.

"Not this time, Every time I understood, I made a decision. Let me inform everyone." AYUSH said.

"Yes, it doesn't matter." Sandeep said.

Ayush, Ankit-Parth tells his girlfriend Divya all. Let's start here, The biggest U-turn of AYUSH's life, Dhruvi Reema and two other men are sitting next to her, Parth is very late, these people talk.

"Come, sit here." Dhruvi said.

"Thank you." AYUSH said.

"What's the matter, yours?" Dhruvi said.

"I don't understand!" AYUSH said.

"Reema doesn't want to So why did the force. Reema, do you want to keep AYUSH as a friend? Getting in a Boyfriend Relationship? You have to live with him. " Dhruvi said.

" The answer is no. " Reema said.

"Then you don't know, Don't bother, You'll know when I slap you. " Dhruvi said.

"No, no, Excessive." AYUSH said.

"Why Excessive, What to say? I will slap here. Reema was very upset with you. " Dhruvi said.

AYUSH thinks in his mind," Same copy to copy is mine. Thinks just like me, The scandal we do, The name comes from another man. Reema must have made a plan And the victim becomes dhruvi. But Duryodhana has to believe Karn, Accompanied without knowing true or false. I wish I had a friend like this. "

That's when Parth arrives, taking his girlfriend.

"Parth, Reema didn't like AYUSH, so why you forcing talk?" Dhruvi said.

"Reema didn't like AYUSH, so why talk for three months?" Parth said.

"She wanted to talk but not move on." Dhruvi said.

"If Dhruvi, we have no interest in anyone, All I know is that Reema doesn't want to join Ayush, So why talk

" Divya said.

"Let's make a mistake, just now." Dhruvi said.

AYUSH thinks in his mind," I committed a crime and you committed mistake! Wahh, Found out today, The girl will be the culprit, If so, do not take any case of the boy, But if there is a case of a girl, the police will crush and kill the boy. Maybe women feel reserved. "

"Now listen, Don't do wrong TIMEPASS now." Dhruvi said.

Hearing this, AYUSH suddenly becomes very angry, started sweating.

"Speaking again." AYUSH said.

"Don't do wrong TIMEPASS now." Dhruvi said.

AYUSH thinks in his mind," Timepass Word felt like an arrow hitting the heart. The meaning of this word should be known. This timepass atleast maybe the current lovers have joined the attraction, love no one. I will search in the details of this word and it will be my new book. "

"What do you think?" Dhruvi said.

"Nothing." AYUSH said.

"Yes, if you have something to say, say it." Parth said.

AYUSH thinks in his mind., "Reema, now you will propose to me, I will bring that time soon And I will prove you wrong. "

"She has a best friend, Somehow you know?" Dhruvi said.

"The answer, Never found. I will never get an answer from my mouth. " AYUSH said.

"Yes, it doesn't matter." Dhruvi said.

AYUSH thinks in his mind.," I felt the timepass tag,

This gives me a lot of trouble, Word. My whole body eats up. I will found answer. Let's new book write start."

[LOVE WAR SEASON 1

DEVIL's RETURN

After reading this part, if any parent is reading my story, ask their son or daughter if they are not playing with someone's life for a while. Because this is a great shame for this society. And maybe I'm sorry to hear that. Because I've seen a lot of this in college myself, I've made up such a mind-boggling story so that it doesn't happen to anyone.

PART 5.1 : (Travel Info)

PART 5.2 : Identification of the book

PART 5.3 : The problem arose

PART 5.4 : The secret between Rahi and Jenil

PART 5.5 : Devil's Return mission

PART 5.6 : Truth

PART 5.7 : LOVE WAR BEGGINING

PART 5.8 : First Final war.

PART 5.1 : (Travel Info)

Time is of the essence,

There is a story in the stories,

There is a mystery in the story itself,

And there is no life in mystery.

Without a reason, even a leaf of a tree cannot move, so this is life. Somehow the reason was hidden in every story when a man is born in the form of a woman or a man. When a bird is flying in the sky, a person standing on the ground says that it has wings by which it flies, when iron is in liquid form, a person says that it has melted due to fire, when a river dries up, a person says There is a lot of rain, when a person who knows such a fact can say such reasons, then why can't such a person speak with a broken heart that the reason may be himself? And if there is a mistake, why blame someone else? Why does the person behave as if there is no fault in the curve? Why is this happening in this society? Why doesn't anyone find a way out of it? And if the road is not paved, why does the person in front suffer in silence? And if there is compulsion, then why the strength of those who are against poverty or saying that there is no support for anyone is greater? Hey bricks also have to be heated to become, when a house becomes a wall and stays strong.

There is such a story, in which the answers to all the questions are hidden.

: - A magic.

No one smiled at the broken heart,

There was no one to wipe away the tears,

The one who left the arrow was wounded,

The rescuer's secret was no.

The magic of words, who can know a special person? The silence of an informed person can also be detrimental to society. Suppose a person is silent after seeing a crime being committed, even if he knows everything, then this person is someone whose silence may be a bigger crime for the society than giving trouble. It has been the case for centuries that it takes a long time to find a crime, but it does not take much time to commit a crime. Even if someone makes such a terrible mistake in seeing and understanding, it becomes magic with time, it was a magic at such a time.

Date: - 05/06/2018

Time 12 minutes past 9 o'clock

A boy, He was walking out of his house, wearing boots, black pants, blue jersey, hair oiled, this boy was walking out of the house he was coming upside down. The scene happened in such a way that the boy was coming upside down suddenly started running as soon as he got out of the house, and slowly increased his speed. he started sweating, eyes started turning red. Sweat rolled down her also, as if he had just come out of the shower, with tears streaming down his also. Everyone on the road was watching him. Now it was time for him to get tired and put his hands on his knees and gasp.

The second scene was something like this, in a house, a boy was standing upside down looking out of the window. A girl was looking at him from behind. So the boy, he was tired of running, took a phone out of his pocket and made a phone call.

"Hello, hello, listen," said the boy, gasping for breath.

"Say." Said the boy standing upside down.

"That, whatever he thought, happened." Said the boy with tears in his eyes.

He cut off the phone to the boy who was in the house and cut the phone to the boy who was on the road and put it in his pocket and said, "We just have to play one game, then the whole world will see the magic, the consequences will be terrible. "

The boy in the house stood up and said, "Now it begins, my story. What I had thought so far came at the behest of someone else, this time only the turn has changed. What was everyone saying? Four or five girlfriends, That the time has come to have a boy friend! Then in such an age I will win and show it. I will answer all those who give nothing but betrayal to those who love them. My name is to not bring darkness in the eyes of those people .... "

Date: 07/02/2018

The time is 11 o'clock in the morning.

There was another character in the story of these two. An expensive car was being driven by a driver, very fast on the road. So he brought a college, a college, inside the car. The driver parked the car outside the office. He got out of the car, got out of the wheelchair, and opened the back door, brought out a girl and put her in the chair. The girl's hand was fractured, her head was hit, maybe that's why she was bandaged, her legs were also hit so she couldn't walk.

Mystery is beginning

The first question is, why did any boy run away?

Question two, what is the story of another boy?

Question 3: Why did you hit a girl so hard?

....

PART 5.2 : Identification of the book

The time that has passed, in which endless things run with darkness,

So there was someone who was tempted to do justice to the truth.

A girl was being taken to the college office by her driver. He came near the office room and opened the door and said something like this. (The gentleman looked like he was wearing a white shirt and black pants, glasses, white hair, and his office table and computer.) That girl's name was Rahi.

"Sir, does Rahi want to meet you? Shall I take them inside?" The driver asked the gentleman sitting inside.

"Yeah yeah, come inside." Mr. said in surprise. "Can Rahi come in alone if his driver?" The question arose in the mind of the Sir.

There the driver brought Rahi inside the room, Sir was surprised to see him and he stood up in his place.

Everything is endless,

What's going on

No one got the time,

The blame has always been on someone.

"Rahi, son, what happened?" The master asked.

"Ankur sir, the reason behind this is that I was born in this college. Sorry, the reason could not be fulfilled here." Rahi replied. (Means sir name Ankur.)

"I mean, something understandable, son of a bitch!" Ankur Sir had a question in his mind as there were no words to understand.

"Sir, do you know Jenil?" Rahi asked Ankur Sir.

"Yeah I know, that star was personal too and mine too." Ankur Sir replied.

"Yeah, that's why it all happened." Rahi said.

"What? A straight boy, whom you accuse of defamation?" Ankur Sir asked with surprise.

"Don't accuse me sir, I just say that he did this, I did not say that it was his fault. He did as he was shown at the time, in which the fault was not his, the fault was mine, sir.

With broken glass, no one asks who broke it! But everyone needs to say so, save it because it will sound a lot. It was glass, but what if we linked it to the heart? So what happens that if the heart is broken, no one asks what happened? But the need is to forget what happened and move on.

Now, sir, let me answer one sentence, whether the heart is broken or the glass, which one day can be reconnected and go to the next time? Maybe I'll just say the answer, no, the answer is no, "said Rahi.

"Tell me all about what you do, the way you let it go today." Ankur said Surrey.

"Sir, look, this is a book with me." Rahi said giving a book to Ankur Sir.

"Which book?" Ankur said holding the book in his hand. "Devil's Return." Said reading the name of the book.

"Yes sir, Devil's Return. The author is Jenil." Rahi said.

"What a debt to this book and to you!" Ankur asked.

"Yes sir, there is a lot to be taken. Perhaps this is written by Janelle to show the true identity of all the young generation of our country India. This helped him to get out of the bus.

Now you may be wondering if it was written? So let me tell you the whole story. And if Jenil's heart is clear and true to you, then spread the word about her book.

We, the ones who decided the controversy unexpectedly,

If trouble befalls him, then we who are in the heart,

A three-inch heart, containing a five-foot man,

An annoying motion, in which the eyes wipe the pillow at night.

It took him a long time to figure out what was really going on. It seemed like the hard work was going wrong. The net was made in such a way that it was decided that it would be salvaged. There was also the author, who turned the whole game around. The players were also at heart, who knew they were going to win, but the winner was always Jenil. Nature gave such a mind that in this life's struggle, if everything went against it, there came a time when it was true. There was a boy whose name was Jenil, who always lived with his love after winning and investing. "Rahi said some things to Jenil.

"Yeah all right, but where is Jenil?" Ankur asked Surrey.

"Jenil is not in this world and I am the one who killed her."
Rahi replied.

"What?" Asked with a standing ovation in his chair.

....

Part 5.3: The problem arose

[Cloud cover, rain forecast,

There is a man sitting in an estimate, waiting.

Now who is waiting in this line? Rain or someone close to the heart? So this sentence can happen in a different way in any situation and it can happen for anyone. But what does this sentence have to do with this story? So that connection was connected in a somewhat different way.]

"What? Janelle isn't in this world?" Ankur sir asked with surprise.

"Yes sir." Rahi replied.

"How? He was teaching everyone to live. So how can this be?" Ankur asked Surrey.

"A saga, Jenil. Let's hear you." Rahi said.

{(Now the storyteller is speaking is entirely in the past.)

One year before today, it will be around 8 o'clock in the morning during the day on 06/02/2018. Jenil came to college. Blue shirt, black pants, black belt, spicy hair, sneaky red mix. Walking slowly came inside the gate of the college, there was nothing like a bag, just a pen in a pressed hand. Inside the college was Jenil whose height was five feet seven inches. Coming in, he put his right hand in his right pants pocket, took his i-card out of his pocket. He held the i-card in his hand to swipe the computer screen, which was swiped and returned to his hand. He walked inside the college. Upon arrival, he searched for the Master of Architect's campus and finally found it. He found his class on campus and came into the class and there were two specimens sitting on the last bench whose names were Neel and Rimal. There were many others but these two were flattering. Now the time has come for something like this in which a big saga has started.

(Architect's class means tables were laid, pictures of houses were on the wall and on the table.)

"Will the girls come if we come?" Neel and Rimal were talking in which Neel came and spoke.

"Our destiny is to make a broken God. We don't even have to pay any respect." Rimal said.

"Finished the whole bachelor architect, but didn't get any. Now it's getting old. This is if another chicken came." Neel said looking in front of Jenil.

Jenil knew that these people were talking to me, so Jenil started walking towards them.

"Ohh, Rimal this is coming to our side." Neel said.

"Steals steals." Rimal said.

"What is theft, let me take such a big man in my pocket! Have some pity, give me a big bag." Neel said.

There Jenil approached him.

"No need to steal, I'm here to steal. Don't think of stealing." Jenil said.

"My loser is smart." Rimal said.

"So be careful man." Jenil said.

"Yeah all right, who and what did you come to steal?" Neel said asking the question.

"College is for studying and having fun, but I've come to steal all these exceptions, arrogance, greed and betrayal from someone's mind. And my name is Jenil." Jenil said.

"Okay, fenil." Neel said.

"Jenil, not Fenil." Rimal said.

"Hey, whatever it is, it's Henil. Listen, you won't find what you came to steal." Neel said.

There, Pooja and Mohini came to the classroom. Then Neel and Rimal looked at us.

"Oh, ah, if two in front, a banger comes." Rimal said looking at the girls.

"Yes, not two, three, three great wars are happening in the heart." Neel said.

"Looking at the girls, the chain of the pants can't stay closed!" Jenil asked in surprise.

"No, don't stay, and you, brother Swami, go to your place. We have to do something that is in class with the girl." Rimal said. Saying this, Janelle came and sat in his place.

My friend and I were looking for our own table. Finding the table my table was attached to Jenil. Finding it, I went to the table and found Jenil sitting with his (Jenil) mouth down and eyes closed. Now something like this happened Jenil slowly raised his mouth and closed eyes. A few tears in his eyes and angry eyes red when he opened his eyes. For a while I panicked what happened to this all of a sudden? But now what does Jenil, whose heart was already broken. Jenil was sitting like that so I went with her.

"Hi." Rahi said.

I asked him hi but he didn't answer. I was skeptical at the time. I stared at him. But he didn't say anything, he didn't even see the point of speaking. Now everything in the class ended with the announcement of Jenil's speech. It's time to go and arrange a room in the hostel. Our college is back in Ahmedabad and we all came from Surat. So a hostel is a must. So when that principal, i.e. Ankur Sir, came to your office, I talked to Jenil.

I was twenty-five feet behind her when Jenil finished her class and walked out to your office.

"Oh, listen. Listen, really." Rahi shouted.

Jenil didn't hear anything. So I ran after him and reached for him.

"Hey you run a lot." Rahi said. But Jenil looked at him and started walking back.

"Hey all the boys try to be heroes at such times and you are the villain!" Rahi said.

"It's just fun to be a villain." Jenil said angrily.

"Well now I'll call you a villain. I don't even know your name. But where are you going?" Rahi asked.

"To set up bed a hostel." Jenil said.

"Well, I have the same job. Let's go together." Rahi said.

So on foot we reached your office.

"Am i the Commissioner. Sorry come in Sir." Jenil said.

"Yes. Why a mistake in speaking like this." Jenil and Rahi were walking inside when Ankur sir said.

"In this girl's babbling circle." Jenil said.

"Hahahahaha, it happens. Tell me what the job was. Sit down first." Ankur sir said.

"Yes sir we had to talk about the hostel." Jenil said.

(At that moment, five students who looked like thugs came into the office room without even asking. There was a Maine student named Jordan. Jordan sat in a chair and put his feet on the table. The other four students were standing.)

"O fuker, I want a room in the hostel." Said Jordan.

"Yes sir set." Ankur sir said. Jenil and Rahi were surprised when Ankur called Jordan Sir.

Jordan looked terribly in front of Rahi.

"Oh Ankur, empty the five rooms around this girl and set us there, or you'll be set." Said Jordan.

Jenil didn't listen to that much.

"I don't really know the girl,

I don't know you after that,

Not able to talk to Sir, and

There is nothing wrong with me breaking your hand to improve, "said Jenil angrily.

"Oh, take it, hero ready too." Said Jordan, standing in his place.

"So I'm ready." Jenil said.

"I'm M.L.A's son and the owner of this college. You can't even count the hours." That's all Jordan said with his hand on Jenil's shoulder.

(Jenil immediately grabbed his hand and struck Jordan's shoulder for the first time, then his shoulder fell off, then the left side of the abdomen attacked the upper part of the kidney and below the ribs with a closed fist. Gone. Then there were the other four students who started beating them too.)

"Do you know who he heated? He will take your life." Ankur sir said.

"I have come back after facing death many times.

Don't try to show okat, "said Jenil.

"I need a student like you. The hostel will be over. You go to the hostel and talk to the rector and get a room. Do the same." Ankur sir said.

Seeing all this, I fell in love with Jenil. Jenil did a terrible blow. When he got angry, I followed him. And we both came out on College Road.

"Oh, he saved me from listening to the villain. So can we become friends?" Rahi said asking the question. With that, Jenil grabbed Rahi's hand and her eyes were red and pushed Rahi a little.

"I'm not here to make a friendship. I'm here for someone whose support I'm the only one at a time like this. I've come here to seek revenge, and I'll be the one to do it. Looks like I've just come to finish it. " Jenil said angrily and Rahi was surprised by such words.

At that moment, Jenil left my hand and headed for the hostel. Jenil looked at someone on the far left. Jenil stood up for a moment and tears welled up in her eyes. There were only red eyes. Seeing that, Jenil started walking forward. So another man who was not recognized also started walking. I chased him but sadly he was suddenly lost somewhere in front of my eyes.

....

PART 5.4 : The secret between Rahi and Jenil

Was lost,

Didn't find anyone,

So what a statue of arrogance he got!

There were some things going on in the current college and some things were incomplete. The story didn't seem so straightforward. It was believed that Jenil was frightened and angry by someone. Only he knew the secret, otherwise everyone's life would have gone on like this. Maybe enemy Jenil wouldn't have been with Jordan.

(Current)

"I mean, Jenil was in a relationship with someone who wouldn't let Jenil live the same way, would you?" Ankur Sir asked the question.

"I felt the same way at the time, but the fact was that no one was in front of me yet, there was just a show going on, just a sacrifice to show someone. Who could not believe it." Rahi said.

(Past)

After the fight, Jenil came out of college with his luggage and books in the hostel. From there he got into a rickshaw and went with a private traveler and after catching the travel he went to Surat. M.L.A. he has this college at her home and the owner of the college was his son Jordan. There he explained everything to Jordan's father.

"Uncle. Nothing else happened to me, but it happened to the girls,,,,,," Jenil said.

"I'll explain it." Said Jordan's dad.

There Jordan came over, and grabbed his left arm with a good hand.

"Dare to come to my house on a date after killing so much?" Said Jordan.

After finishing all this, Jenil left and reached the hostel at that time, just not to talk to anyone. When he reached the hostel after eating, there were two other students in his room who were not even paying attention while talking. He just fell asleep keeping his mind alone. It will be about 20 minutes past 9 o'clock.

After a while, Jenil started having dreams, there was something in the dream that made Jenil go away. There were many men too. Going to the crematorium and seeing the anxiety burning, the tears in his eyes that were seen in his dreams were now really in his eyes. All of a sudden he woke up. Rahi, Pooja and Mohika, on the other hand, were awake in three rooms, all in one room.

"What a fierce battle Jenil did!" Said Rahi thinking.

"You didn't fall for it, did you?" Pooja asked.

"Yes it is but it deals with something inverted." Rahi said.

"Inverted way, I don't understand!" Mohika asked with surprise.

"That means something different is happening to him. There's something in the past that Jenil is very anxious to remember. Even though it's the first time I've met him, he's still misbehaving with me." Rahi said.

"He may not have a love affair. If the number is his, call and annoy him, maybe he will hold both your words and your hand!" Mohika said.

"You're right. I'll call him." Rahi said thinking.

There he calls Jenil, and there Jenil laughs a little and receives the call.

[Question: Jenil was so annoyed, now why did smile look at the phone and pick up the phone?]

"I speak Rahi, Jenil." Rahi said.

"Yes the number is saved, I did save too." Jenil said.

(Dialogue Jenil's and Rahi's.)

"Yes, I did not like your behavior today."

"It simply came to our notice then."

"So what else can you do to solve those problems by talking to me?"

"It never ends. And I can't even say that."

"No matter, I won't even ask you about it, villain."

"The villain said he would never try to be a hero."

"Why are you treating me like that?"

"I'm just coming."

"So you stop talking to me about something like this."

"It will never stop. You need a true heart to understand. I will tell you only if it appears to me."

"I mean, you haven't seen it in me yet."

"Yeah didn't show up."

"Don't worry, get a little cold. Right now we're just talking, not fighting. We'll only get to know each other by talking."

"No, I recognize it for the first time."

"Yeah. So how am I?"

"I'll let you know when the time comes."

"Yes, it doesn't matter. I'll be ready."

The conversation went on like this and finally the conversation stopped and both of them hung up the phone.

"What's going on?" Mohika asked.

"I don't think this comes to mind." Rahi said.

"I will start trying to bring it into the conversation," Pooja said.

"After talking about being in love for six or seven months, he doesn't realize that we have to change boys too?" Rahi said. Then Pooja and Mohika were amazed by these words.

"You mean you want to be in a relationship for a few days?" Pooja said.

"Yeah Al that sounds pretty crap to me, Looks like boyfriend for me either." Rahi said.

"You're doing it wrong, Rahi." Pooja said.

"Please don't talk about this anymore." Rahi said joining hands. "It's too late now. You go to sleep and let me sleep too."

Talking like this, Rahi was getting ready to go to sleep and when she came out of the worship room and called someone, it was none other than Jenil. Their dialogue.

"Hello Jenil!"

"Rahi planned to pass the time, total betrayal and timepass."

"How did you know Rahi was doing a timepass?"

"My game has started now," Jenil said with a smile.

"What a game."

"The game I've been waiting for. Now Rahi is so entangled in the whole game that she can't even get out."

"What are you able to do?"

"You want me to talk to the rector so you can come to the football field."

"Yes I'm ready to come."

Thus put down the phone.

[Question: What is the relationship between Pooja and Jenil?]

....

PART 5.5 Devil's Return mission

Talk about rubbing salt in my wounds bad smile!

Say no to believing, which is why no sacrifice was made.

Pooja was found on the football field at Jenil's request.

"How are you, sister?" Jenil asked.

"Now I really don't know what's going on in your mind." Pooja also asked a question in reply.

"Yes sister explain the move." Jenil said.

(Past also within the past.)

Six months ago today, my friend Dewang came to our house. Omkar and I were sitting when Dewang came home. [It is to be reminded here that in the first part, the boy who ran upside down outside the house and called someone is this Omkar] Dewang coming home. I was sitting on the sofa with my laptop and Omkar was sitting next to me.

"Hi, How are you friends?" Dewang at home.

"Ohh, you appeared brown after so many days." Jenil said.

"After many days, even a few days in a brotherhood can take years." Said Omkar.

"Talk to you soon and keep up the good content." Dewang said.

"Yes, man, he is not someone's relative. Brothers and sisters should be taken care of in time and when the time comes, help should also be given to the family." Jenil said.

"Yeah dude it hurts." Dewang said.

"No problem, brother. This is like a legacy that must be preserved." Jenil said.

"Yes it is. Tell me what else goes on." Said Omkar.

"Hey, I said I'll meet my girlfriend when I come! It's 10 o'clock now. She'll be in the garden right now." Dewang said.

"Let's go, and party today from Dewang." Jenil said.

Then the three of us set out to go to the garden. While talking, we reached the garden and looked at someone from Dewang. And Dewang was suddenly amazed. It was as if a girl was sitting with a boy.

"Who does Rahi connect with?" He spoke to Dewang with a question in his mind.

"Oh, I don't think his brother will do anything." Jenil said.

"No. I am his brother." Omkar said with surprise. Saying this, Dewang and Jenil became very serious.

"What mean! Who is there?" Dewang said.

Then my eyes went to someone else. (Present time : night Jenil and Pooja meeting football Ground.)

Pooja can't say no right now as it is not in my planning. Then I was more angry than Dewang. Because the trouble was too much for me. Dewang then went to both of them. Then the girl suddenly stood up. And that girl was none other than Rahi.

(Again Past situation.)

"Who is this?" Dewang asked.

"My new boyfriend Sandeep." Rahi said.

"So you're betraying me." Dewang said.

"Yeah. If you haven't meet me yet, I'll be with someone else." Rahi replied.

"Let's not talk about this. Let's go." Sandeep said.

Then Rahi and Sandeep left. But Dewang suddenly started crying terribly. And persuading him but losing his patience and he went home without saying anything and me and Omkar also went home. Then at 11 o'clock at night I got a call from Dewang.

(Dewang and Jenil's dialogue.)

"I speak Dewang."

"Yes, brother, you are suddenly gone."

"I'm leaving everyone now." Dewang spoke so much that I thought he would do something on his own.

"Listen brother, I'm with you. Don't go down the road thinking of something. I'll save you."

"No, the brother you dreamed of is not with him."

"You're standing at home. I'm just like that." I kept calling as soon as I felt something was wrong and I immediately ran as our society had a house after thirteen houses. As soon as I got there, I shot him in the head and committed suicide.

(A past back.) Second present : Football ground.

"What does Jenil say. Dewang is not in this world?" Pooja said.

"Yes. The phone was on and there was a terrible noise in front of the ear and it took its own life. We took it to the crematorium and we were standing together when it was burning to ashes. As it burned the tears from my and Omkar's eyes. Because we believed more than brother. And in front of us he committed suicide. Totally fake love. Totally timepass. (Angry situation) Many such people may have been martyred in this timepass cycle and I am playing this game to show the world to stop it. When I was young, my mouth was burning with firecrackers and everyone was calling me a zombie. When I was in a lot of trouble, only Dewang used to call me a devil. That is why the name of this game and the name of the mission is Devil Return. The Devil returns to save someone's side, Devil returns. After me, everyone will know that when you give trouble to someone without bending, what kind of game is being played in front of them. War is necessary because it is a shame even for the parents of these people. Yeah will learn love from me, Otherwise will meet death, just like many people have committed suicide, they will also have to life line. The rest of this battle will be about the Devil's Return mission. "Jenil spoke angrily.

Jordan stood behind him and listened.

After reading this part, if any parent is reading my story, ask their son or daughter if they are not playing with someone's life for a while. Because this is a great shame for this society. And maybe I'm sorry to hear that. Because I've seen a lot of this in college myself, I've made up such a mind-boggling story so that it doesn't happen to anyone.

....

PART 5.6 : Truth

There was a house that is no longer there,

Begging, begging, screaming,

He could not survive after doing everything.

Jordan heard this and walked over to him.

"The stories are super. Just maybe I can make her a character to defend someone in that story Jenil?" Told Jordan with remorse after hearing everything.

"Yes brother, now you also have to be a part because all these things were known to Pooja today except me and Omkar, what you have come to know so now you also have to understand." Jenil said.

"Got it, you go ahead, I'm with you from now on." Said Jordan.

The next morning Rahi Pooja was with Jenil.

"Villain, it's over now. I like you. It's better not to bother now." Rahi said.

"Never mind, I'll take revenge when I have to. We're both friends now." Jenil said.

"I don't know what you want to do. But stay with me as long as you are." Rahi said.

There was Sandeep's call on Rahi's phone which she was cutting, seeing this Jenil smiled a little in her mind. He felt that now Rahi was falling in love with Jenil.

"Whose phone was it?" Janelle said.

"No one, let alone all that. The villain was good to meet you and the big thing is that you got admission in Master Architect." Rahi said.

After saying this, Jenil looked at Pooja and Pooja felt a sting of something and she was thinking something like this in her mind. "Jenil has a bachelor's degree in civil engineering, so why not a master's degree in civil engineering? Why an architect?"

The conversation went on like this, and Rahi had to go out with some paperwork so Pooja called Jordan and Jenil. They all went up to terrace.

"I know Pooja has a question in your mind." Jenil said.

"Yeah that makes sense to me." Pooja said.

"Listen. When Dewang was among us, I asked Omkar to give me admission in this college. So when Rahi was at his house, he got admission. Said the phone.

(It is to be remembered that the boy who ran away in the first part was Omkar and the one who called him was Jenil. Jenil was at home with his sister.) Then Jordan is no bad man he was already in this planning. I knew Jordan owns this college. Before the owner he was my special friend who we studied together. But the bachelor left us. I told Jordan to come to the office and treat him badly and I would fight him. That is, I became a hero in Rahi's eyes when Jordan attacked the office at my behest. I needed to get closer to Rahi to complete Dewang's revenge, "Jenil explained the whole plan.

"But there's still a man you're afraid of." Pooja asked.

"Yeah but this time is not perfect and cant's said this past." Jenil said.

....

PART 5.7 : LOVE WAR BEGGINING

I won the big fight,

It was a big forest,

The name of the loser was with,

Although someone in love was attached.

While they were waiting for a different time on terrace, something different happened.

"Now thinking of a game, Jenil?" Asking the question said Pooja.

"Yes, Sandeep is going to go to Rahi's house tomorrow. Jordan will go to his house at the same time Sandeep is there. Only time will tell when I will go to save Rahi. It will be time to remind Rahi of Dewang. And you are talking about a different man and I am afraid. His story will start tomorrow. It will be very difficult to turn the story upside down, but it will also be necessary to end the war in which my mistake has become a topic of discussion in the world that needs to be completed. " Jenil said the whole thing.

"One thing to keep in mind, Jenil, who has a way of war to improve everything in her mind, never wanted to do anything wrong. Jenil, I think you are innocent somewhere." Said Jordan.

"Whether I am innocent or not is a different matter, but the culprits are my own men whom I kept in my heart. That was my timstake, brother. Maybe if I had used my brain there, I could have caught those people today. And last but not least. "Whether I am innocent or not is a different matter, but the culprits are my own men whom I kept in my heart. That was my mistake, brother. Maybe if I had used my brain there, I could have caught those people today. And last but not least. Proved these people to kill dewang. So from there my game started, people were playing and sitting there were more people who used brains. And I will show those people the fire of hatred alone. " Jenil said.

So from there my game started, people were playing and sitting there were more people who used brains. And I will show those people the fire of hatred alone. " Jenil said.

"It doesn't matter, let's give justice to Dewang first." Said Jordan.

"But the first phase of the war will end tomorrow and then the second war will be the final war. This is not a Mahabharata that eighteen phases have to be made, this war is to save the society but this war is only to take the youth power in the right direction. Jordan, get out now, I'll get there too. We'll finish the war at the perfect time by setting up a place to stay right around Rahi's house. The Devil's Return is the name of the game. Let's finish it first." Jenil said.

"Yeah, I'll get out." Said Jordan.

All these people were waiting in the area around Rahi at night, Rahi was seen talking to someone late at night whose Jenil and Jordan knew but Omkar was passing these words to these people. The next morning, shortly after, Sandeep came to his house and was sitting next to Rahi, laughing and gesturing to him and Jenil Jordan to go home. Jordan went to his house and then something like this happened ....

"Then you jumped a lot today with someone else?" Jordan was told to come home and Rahi was surprised and Sandeep was also sitting with his mouth down.

"Jordan, are you here? Get out of here. Your idea is too bad." Rahi said.

"I'm not going to get rid of the chickens sitting next to you, today is the day to spend with you." Said Jordan.

"I felt like I was walking between you. I'm going to save you. Suddenly I remembered a lot of work." Sandeep said.

"But this Jordan has come to annoy me to save me!" Rahi said.

"Oh, I'll save you if I'm save self defend but i can's self defend.. And why don't I take such trouble for you." Sandeep said.

"It doesn't matter if there is a man present who will do his duty." Jenil said coming home.

"You save me. I don't need to take trouble." Sandeep said.

Sandeep got out of there and Jordan also got angry and looked at Jenil. Going out, Jordan came out with a smile on his face and sighed.

"Jenil, let me tell you something today. I was a boy for Sandeep today, I left him and Sandeep didn't even have time to save me. I miss Dewang very much today." When Rahi said that, Jenil got a hashtag and laughed in his mind. It now occurred to Jenil that Rahi had lost everything in her mind to betray the since that was running through her mind.

"I'll send his a photo and an address. Will you come and tell me?" Rahi asked.

"Yes, I will take you to see you tomorrow morning." Jenil said.

"Thank you." Rahi said.

"Come on dude let's talk, your brain will divert." Jenil said.

Talking like this, everything came to an end and in the evening Jenil went to the garden where Sandeep and his brothers were sitting who called Jordan to give justice. (It is to be reminded here that this game was of the Second [season 2: coming soon] War, so it will be revealed later how the first War came to be.)

The next day, Jenil took Rahi in an expensive car, saying that he should take Dewang with him. The thing is, there is no Dewang. So Rahi sit on near driver sheet was driving in a dry place.

"Thank you Jenil." Rahi said.

"Get Dewang first, then there's no time to say thank you." Jenil said.

"You mean I don't understand?" Rahi asked.

"Because I am a special brother of Dewang and the revenge that came was with you." Rahi was terrified because Jenil was so angrily said.

"If you want to meet Dewang, take it." Jenil said and Rahi's part hit the car with the road roller at high speed and hit Rahi hard but Jenil's heart stopped.

....

PART 5.8 : First Final war.

Times became very difficult,

There was no such thing

Which is not even to say today.

After the accident, Rahi was taken to the hospital and after recovering, she came to Ankur Sir immediately.

(Present situation. Ankur sir and Rahi both meeting.)

"I started to hate Jenil, but Jordan brought Jenil's book and told me to read it, then I found out the fact." Rahi said.

"Now Jenil?" Ankur said.

"Not in this world." Rahi said.

There soon Jenil came from behind and Rahi was surprised. Now the big thing is that later another brother also came with Jordan. It was Dewang. Seeing this, the ground slipped from Rahi's feet as Dewang was killed.

"Are you a live?" Rahi asked in surprise.

"Yes." Dewang said.

"So, then who committed suicide?" Rahi asked.

There Dewang put his hand on Jenil's shoulder and reassured him.

"Brother, if it is good to forget what happened, don't forget the truth, tell everything that is filling your mind today." Dewang said.

(The whole story that Jenil will tell will be very painful.)

"When Dewang went to hurt himself, there was another man with him. She is also in trouble. I still believe he has a girlfriend whose name was Khushi. My Khushi.

When Rahi was sitting in the garden you were with Sandeep, he was engaged to Khushi, when we came to the garden I was more angry as Khushi was also present and I saw her. That was my pleasure. Khushi also called me when Dewang's phone rang on me at night, but I called Dewang with Divert Omkar and I went to save Khushi. But before I could reach that fan.......... She is committed suicide. Trouble is with me, maybe we can try to save a man if she is alive in front of us, but with two or three minutes of deep thought, a man is lost among us that we are nothing without her. I have lived every single word I wrote in the Devil's Return Book. You just look at the story in words, I have feel those words. It is said that an incomplete story happens to many people but no character in an incomplete story leaves the world forever, even Sandeep has to suffer from this. Rahi has understood over time but there is no one to judge my happiness now except me and I will continue to give.

We were talking about a story like this,

feel forever, tear forever, I can't understood, and justice self.

Today I miss her a lot Dewang, yes I enjoyed the fight, love was also to be overcome, but someone to fight like this? What happens right? And if there was someone else's guilt behind all this, I would have forgiven Omkar, but the guilt behind all this is Omkar. "Jenil pulled the gun out of his pocket and killed Omkar. Which is hard to contain. [It seems to read the story carefully from the end to the end.]]

"Yes, this type story written by me. Season second part Then think next time." AYUSH think in mind.

....

Part 6 : AYUSH begins the examination of his own life.

Thoughts are running through Ayush's mind, No way to go to that hostel and now college. Which mouth should I go to? But now i has to go to the hostel. Parth meet AYUSH.

"What are you doing?" AYUSH said.

"Hey, I have to go home. Divya and I have some work to do. If you tell me that, why don't you say something? " Parth said.

"Someone stopped me." AYUSH said.

"Who was that?" Parth said.

"I wouldn't say name but she was a college professor." AYUSH said.

"It's means, Will also be known in engineering." Parth said.

"Yes." AYUSH said.

"Listen, You don't do anything upside down until I do, Be careful. We have to forget what happened now. " Parth said.

" No, you have to remember. Dhruvi left one thing in my mind while speaking. My whole mind is always there. " AYUSH said.

"Listen, In the hostel, All It is known. " Parth said.

" Impression is already a gene process. Don't worry." AYUSH said.

"Yes, right. Many people said that even though the whole hostel knows, Ankit has refused to create an atmosphere that makes you feel sad. Assuming that is your backup. Come on, I'm late, I have to go. " Parth said.

Now that Ayush's brain has stopped running, he goes to Jordan's room.

" Let's Jordan, play chess. " AYUSH said.

"Every time you win, You teach me." Jorden said.

"The brain is stopped, Maybe chess is a relief! " AYUSH said.

Jordan listens intently as AYUSH murmurs in his mind with playing chess.

"Elephant straight, Camel torment, Horse and a half, Wazir anywhere. The Wazir is called the queen. (Suddenly thought comes to mind.) Jordan I have a work right now, i will meet you." AYUSH said.

Jordan thinks to himself. "What happen? Can't speak AYUSH, But it is better not to do anything wrong. "

AYUSH goes to the room. The laptop opens And searches, Suicide case of a boy or girl between the ages of fifteen and twenty-five. It doesn't have the perfect figure, Yet 37861 cases came to India in three months, In it, 975 couples have committed suicide, The rest is different girl boy.

AYUSH think in mind."If there is such a period, The rest are killed separately, So he/she may have received love and betrayal. Have some college study tension. This means that even 500 of them have committed suicide due to betrayal in love. And being happy of someone Betrayer, may mean TIMEPASSED. That's why Dhruvi goes to compare me with those people. Of these, many couples break up every day. Only a few commit suicide, No no no, not love, LOVE IS TIMEPASS. Suicide case is very high. whole life would have been spent on his/her own life. Now there is no way to stop this timepass. This is a poison that spreads in the college. This poison will be poured on someone on a daily basis and someone will be kill. The poison that was tolerated happened And what didn't happen is gone. This poison cannot be stopped Because this toxin has already spread. Let's now remove TIMEPASS tag. Nothing else to do, The world has gone to great lengths."

It's been a few days. The hostel has a sports ground, gym and swimming pool for students. So five or six people have to take a swimming. Adjacent to it is a basketball ground adjacent to the swimming pool. That means the boys in the hostel have to come in swimming clothes. At that time girls were playing basketball on the basketball ground. And these people came to Reema's notice. And all boy ragging to AYUSH. The next afternoon Parth calls Ayush to the hostel and talks.

"Yes, why did you call me here?" AYUSH said.

"Brother, the matter with the swimming pool has become very big." Parth said.

"What happened?" AYUSH said.

"If Rima had told Dhruvi at night ....

[

I was told by Direct dhruvi to come to college and say," Parth you are not aware at all, Reema started crying in front of me because of what you did in the swimming pool.

"Don't say anything to Parth. Everything will be bad." Divya said.

"What's going to get worse?" Dhruvi said. So much so that Dhruvi through bottle in front Divya. The two came face to face.

]

"You made a mistake, not in a hostel, but in college." AYUSH said.

"College, that is!" Parth said.

AYUSH slowly gets angry and said," Reema didn't like the first point, So what a tent camp on a two-hour basketball field made! Reema pretended to cry and got this fight done. Do not have the strength to speak for reema's yourself, My anger is exacerbated by calling from the Dhruvi's teachings. Don't be quiet now: there will be a big first, Slap me by talk dhruvi, Then she said no timepass withe reema. You are only a very smart girl! Were we the champions to make Aligarh parrots? Now bring me face to face. No more fear. I'm going to your college, To finish everything. Reema calls us Dhruvi and goes to scare us, She does not know that I am a star in this field. Let's go fast. "

"AYUSH calms down, If increase your anger, your brain will not work. Our guilt happened a little bit."Parth said.

" We don't, You and other student. I did not speak the name out of my mouth. And the thing is, she didn't like it, Butch was to be killed for two hours! That answer is also needed, she goes to press another people. For the first time in my life, I liked a girl, its bad situation creation. If i Was living alone, its good life. Life was stress free." AYUSH said.

"But now everything is under control." Parth said.

"How?" AYUSH said.

" Your friend Sandeep came and stopped. And speaking, if anything happened to AYUSH, there would be no one worse than me. It means everyone has fought in your support. Reema was left alone. Sandeep is sadder than what happened in the canteen. Those people (Reema and dhruvi) are hitting the ax on their feet. You can't go and stop them. Everything is fine and under control. In the eyes of all, you are a very cool man And Kishan Pandya said to Dhruvi that 'AYUSH is the best man with a calm mind.' You are going to break the trust of those people. Understand and take action, don't angry. I didn't say all this But Sandeep says me can speak, If you find out later, it will be lot happen. " Parth said.

"That's what we call Kishan PK. How does he know me? " AYUSH said.

"Yes , Everybody got to know you from Annual Function. " Parth said.

"But I'm not going to sit still this time. Reema goes to suppress us, Threatening cry to frighten others, Don't match here." AYUSH said.

"Yes, it doesn't matter." Parth said.

Then Parth tells Sandeep everything, Now AYUSH is with Reema's class, So what to understand?

....

Part 7 : AYUSH's entry into architecture

AYUSH thinks on the way from hostel to college." Parth says that Sandik and PK and many others stood by me and spoke. Opposite them despite being in their class. Both of these seem a bit daunting. When there was a commotion in the canteen, Sandeep said settle in class. If I send a sorry message to Reema on Facebook twenty five times maybe she will call me. Now is the chance to go into architecture. "

AYUSH then To do the message, And no one is aware of this, This means that Reema and Dhruvi know that now all support will come to AYUSH.

This is how the August month comes. Since it is an independent day, the hostel pyramid has to be performed, After leaves, All student thinks of sitting down all night and having a party for the junior of the hostel.

"Everyone gave a great performance today, You really built a pyramid about India and gave a new passion to the newcomer student of the hostel, It was a great performance. Now I call everyone because you are going to have a fresher's party, So this time the boy will have a party with the girl in the auditorium. But yes, don't bet by looking at the girl, Because then we will also celebrate Rakshabandhan. And the girlfriend he was going to make could also be a sister. " Ankit said.

This makes AYUSH a little happy. AYUSH think in his mind," The setting we do instead of guarding. Thank you Ankit. Now the schedule will be decided, My name will be in the suspense dance, I will decide after that, Let's get back to work. "

AYUSH enrolled in suspense dance, In which the name of the song is not given first, The name of the song will be given on the day performance. Parth is called to the room.

"To be able to dance! " Parth said.

"Yes, I will dance." AYUSH said.

"Which song?" Parth said.

"I don't want to leak the song right now. Don't even tell you in the girl hostel. "

" AYUSH said.

"I won't say no." Parth said.

"Mitesh is the dancer of our hostel, I will practice with him." AYUSH said.

Party 24/08/2017

Now the day comes when all the fresher's party performances are done, It is the turn of AYUSH, The song is 'broken angle' Then all the performances were over, and Garba started and finally the disco.

AYUSH goes to Mitesh's room the next day where Parth and many others are sitting. And talking.

"After watching the dance, the CR of the architect has decided that Mitesh, you come to teach dance. " Parth said.

"Brother, I am not going to come that way. Ayush, you will come. " Mitesh said.

"No, very dangerous." Parth said.

"I to talk to about coming to the architect but whose talk man?" AYUSH said.

"Akshay name." Parth said.

"Entry will be found, I will play whatever song I can dance. " AYUSH said.

"Take the entry first." Parth said.

"Before tomorrow evening I'll be at the Architect, If you want to keep writing, keep writing. " AYUSH said.

"Ok." Parth said.

Ayush leaves and calls Sandeep instead of Akshay.

"I don't know if Mitesh will come or not. I will come." AYUSH said.

"You'll be here by evening." Sandeep said.

"Now I will call Akshay." AYUSH said.

AYUSH calls Akshay.

"Hello Akshay, I am AYUSH." AYUSH said.

"Yes." Akshay said.

"If Mitesh wants another man, can I come?" AYUSH said.

"I have to ask Reema. " Akshay said.

"Why?" AYUSH said.

"Reema has to perform herself." Akshay said.

"Ok, Replay me fast." AYUSH said.

After a while, Akshay gets a call back.

"You can come." Akshay said.

"Thanks dude, tomorrow at four o'clock." AYUSH said.

What AYUSH wanted was slowly happening.

AYUSH thinks in his mind."It will be fun now. I will get everything from Reema. Yes, it is."

....

Part 8 : AYUSH's love story continues.

7/09/2017

Now timepass also means tearing up a letter, And AYUSH fell in love. AYUSH is very happy that he is going to be an architect. And he has found that Reema has to learn dance too, And the teacher is both Mitesh and AYUSH, What happens now?

It's four o'clock in the evening, Mitesh and AYUSH went for tea and breakfast, but nothing happened to AYUSH.

"It's first time lot happen." Mitesh said.

"No, it's nothing." AYUSH said.

"Brother, I am an experienced player. " Mitesh said.

"Yes, yes, I know your conspiracy. Let's move on now. " AYUSH said.

He drank tea and went to the architect. Eight girls, three couples, Two girls, This way the dance was to be taught on different songs in three groups. Then those who had to learn were waiting on the terrace. Both of them went (AYUSH and Mitesh.). But AYUSH did not see Reema at all. Now the first task was to teach eight girls, It had a position Reema from the center to the left. Continued to teach dance. First Mitesh sat down and continued AYUSH. Reema didn't know there so she went to talk to him.

"I don't know what to do, show it again!" Reema said.

"I'm sorry, I'm not allowed, To teach you, So Mitesh will teach you. " AYUSH said.

Mitesh think in his mind." Who refuses to teach? "

Ayush said in his mind but Mitesh understood the gesture that way. "You will not react at all. I know, No one said no, But right now I don't know her, it's situation creation."

"Ok. I can teach you." Mitesh said.

After two or three minutes.

"Give me two minutes so I can drink some water." Reema said.

An hour has not yet come reema. But practice what AYUSH has taught, There Ayush and Mitesh talk about slow.

"After two minutes, she went for a walk in the Taj Mahal. " AYUSH said.

"Don't go for a walk in the Taj Mahal, Whether you will build the Taj Mahal or not, she went out to find the answer. " Mitesh said.

"Escape from you too. " AYUSH said.

"One works, You go downstairs to drink water. You must have been thirsty for an hour. " Mitesh said.

"I can't even get water. " AYUSH said.

"I know I'm telling you to act."Mitesh said.

"So let's get to work. You learn to dance, I work. " AYUSH said.

AYUSH goes downstairs and Reema is sitting alone. AYUSH stands a little farther away. Reema walks in front of him But AYUSH moves away. Suddenly Reema joined him.

"You taught and Miteshbhai also taught. Nothing penetrates the mind." Reema said.

AYUSH said with a slight increasing heartbeat." Now if you come down, drink water."

A girl in front of AYUSH takes a bottle and drinks water without speaking and the girl speaks.

"Finished the whole bottle." One girl said.

"So the dance was very difficult." AYUSH said.

"Water Filled with washbasins. " One girl said.

AYUSH said in mind. "Insult."

Now he is very happy to see Reema smiling. He then becomes Reema's personal dancer. Now it happens that Mitesh went to the side of the dance and fell alone.

" AYUSH, I am tired of learning. " Mitesh said.

"We will see. " AYUSH said.

"I saw you before I wanted anything." Mitesh said.

"Brother, do you understand for whom I came? I do my work. " AYUSH said.

"No, no, no problem, Understand AYUSH. " Reema said.

It's time to leave the college, But AYUSH can't go. These were the last days of AYUSH to laugh.

....

Part 9 : Reema proposed

19/09/2017

AYUSH went to Architect, What would have happened from 7/09/2017 till today? What days would have been? What would AYUSH be thinking in his mind. And somehow he came to Ankit's room and said that he must have saved everything.

"Hey AYUSH, come on, what happened? You were going to the architect. I got the news, I met you many days." Ankit said.

"It is eleven o'clock now and I am getting a good night's sleep. But now it seems time. " AYUSH said.

"It's happen." Ankit said.

"What I wanted will happen but I will not get what I wanted. " AYUSH said.

"I don't understand, what are you talking about?" Ankit said.

"Let me explain the whole thing to you. Everywhere you look today, the tide of protectionist sentiment is flowing. It just so happened that we were talking face to face architects, If it was new then I would also enjoy a little talk. Comedy also runs. But I washed my hands of some things. Something like this happened while we were talking on the phone.

[(Past situation)

"Why does Reema love you dance? Why don't you just talk to me now and practice?" AYUSH said.

"I will practice in front of you too."Reema said.

"If you have taken this song well, you can dance comfortably, pay a little attention. " AYUSH said.

"It would be fun if I sang the song. "Drink and dance." ."Reema said.

"Hey ...... (then starts breathing loudly) then he makes you sing such a song."AYUSH is immediately taken aback.

"Yes, what's in it?" Reema said.

"I tried to calm the blood pressure up." AYUSH said. "It's a collection of some poetry, if anything, tell me." Reema said.

"The world is boiling in this little thing,

Wherever there is a wave, there is a talk,

The one that is surviving,

People living together even after a fight,

Doesn't seem to have left any sacrament!

And that's the answer,

Let's stay together,

Sorry if i feel a little wrong,

We are pure in heart,

Do not use the brain in relationships,

Maybe this is our strength,

That we live in everyone's heart! " AYUSH said.

"Hey, you're a great writer." Reema said.

"Thank you." AYUSH said.

The time has come for bad things to happen.

Will it be his information, maybe his own away from us,

I will meet him, maybe that will be the victory or defeat of my life.

"Shall I tell you something?" Reema said.

"So far so good. say" AYUSH said.

"You know, Divyesh (best friend) knows whatever I do. I will not do anything without asking him, He must know anything. " Reema said.

"Ok. it means canteen matter?" AYUSH said.

"Yes, he knows everything." Reema said.

"So what does private talk mean?" AYUSH said.

"Nothing like that for the two of us. We both need to talk. " Reema said.

"Does that tell you what happened all day?" AYUSH said.

"If I had a chance to speak." Reema said.

"If he refuses to talk in the future, will you?" AYUSH said.

"No, what do I do?" Reema said.

"What if I get in trouble?" AYUSH said.

"If there is a problem, nothing will happen, Divyesh will not give me thinking, I tell his all about talking to someone and saying yes to anyone. Don't go for less that your full potential. "

](Present)

"Ankit bro, is on top of me and the darkness is broken. Who has no father in it, Who is not his brother, Who is not a boy of his uncle, With whom there is no relation except friend, This Reema is sitting giving his the right to do what he says. Now I wonder what would happen if timepass happened. Life becomes hell. Now she will propose to me only if he says so. Totally do timepasses by Reema. Reema's heart is not moving or her brain.I think if she wakes up tomorrow and goes on a honeymoon with someone, she will talk about it in detail. Reema, who gave such a right, did not say anything even at home. Now if I want to talk about anything, I have to do it with Divyesh. And I don't think Reema would have been the first if someone had given her the right to do so. Today my whole life will be on me, At first I thought that if I live alone, I would have an idea like this, if I was talking to someone alone? Someone will be. One hundred percent I am not the first. And after seeing all this, in a few days I felt that I would get the answer I thought. And from the bottom of my heart I did not want the answer to be what I thought it would be. Now an hour ago.

[(Past)

"Why did you suddenly remember I went all day, now the message came." AYUSH said.

"Don't talk too much. I'm speaking directly. You are in my heart." Reema said.

AYUSH thinks in his mind, "This too must have told him. She has been given his right throughout his life. And says am in the heart. Don't make such jokes. You don't have a thing called heart and brain and if there is, it will be closed. It's just a timepass, but before the breakup, I'll give you ideas that you can think of for the rest of your life and understand the world. "

"I don't understand!" AYUSH said.

"I love you." Reema said.

"I love you, too." AYUSH said.

](Present)

"Ankit bro, who gave the right to someone else, what to do. PK Sandeep and many others rejected reema, I don't know. I didn't believe her. He also said that even if he explain it to me, I will not understand.

Reema call myself mature but She have not a whole brain and heart." AYUSH said.

....

Part 10 : AYUSH's Game Start.

19/09/2017

So far it was that, AYUSH thought that, Just think of the tag timepass, Now this fight was becoming a matter of life. The hand of the one whom she loves also touches the hand of another. A man who is an operating machine.

Now the machine can run as the man says but it can run as fast as it knows from start to turn off.

"Why, you're surprised!" Reema said.

Even though AYUSH has doubts, he speaks as if he knows. "Edge, all of a sudden he proposed to me."

"But I don't want to be in a relationship wrong so I'll tell you one thing." Reema said.

"True, there should be no problems in the relationship." AYUSH said.

"I had a boyfriend before you, i.e. three or four months ago, but there was a breakup. Don't get me wrong. I don't even think about it anymore." Reema said.

AYUSH is getting happy with what he thought came true and said. "We will forget anything. Every now and then the car explodes like the Research Department of Explosives. "

"I don't understand." Reema said.

"RDX bomb, this is the bomb that exploded in my heart many times. I'll call you RDX now. " AYUSH said.

AYUSH said in mind. ""Which will then be known simply as X." Feeling weird.

"I want to name you after the dialogue." Reema said.

"Everybody loves us, but the mistake is that the villain never gets heroin." AYUSH said.

(Now Ankit and Ayush are sitting.) Present.

"Named the villain, it's all right. " AYUSH said.

"But it doesn't matter if it works?" Ankit said.

"But I know I'm going to have a breakup, but I'm still a man, Who will live with it. Love admits that even though it is wrong. He wants to be with her even though he knows everything. Not to meet but to hope. Oh, if there is such love, I should not do it." AYUSH said.

"I will not say that. If something goes wrong, Teach will be found. " Ankit said.

"It's not, it's just that Parth Jill Jordan Mitesh and some other people know what Reema knows?" AYUSH said.

"I don't understand?" Ankit said.

"As you can see, we all planned to name Reema. Details of what we people are doing in the hostel. I attend twenty-four hours for study or any work. If anything works. Why did he know all that and told me on the phone to wake up at three o'clock. All this Parth tells Divya and she conveys the whole thing to Reema. We think the word reaches us but all the talk of Boy Hostel has reached there in Girl Hostel. Now, when the time comes, if anything happens to Parth, the time will come when he will leave with only the girl and the other thing is that all the other friends are on her side. " AYUSH said.

"Why do you think that?" Ankit said.

"That's why I came to your room, Before that I went to Parth's room to give this news, I just told his that I proposed, Then he told everyone, So those people said that now just leave the night out. And Parth supported him in this. Tell me, girls, is it a toy? " AYUSH said.

"Everyone thinks so?" Ankit said.

"Yes, and teach me back, I just came to hear. It is because of such people that this society has changed, By now the girls will be timepassing with the boys. If there are such people then these people timepass with girls. It sounds bitter, But such people attack the dignity of good girls." AYUSH said.

"What do you want?" Ankit said.

"If we are going to have a breakup, I love it, then I thought of a plan to save it. REVENGE FOR TIMEPASS. REVENGE FOR BROKEN HEART, REVENGE FOR CURRENT CULTURE." AYUSH said.

[SEASON 1 COMPLETED.]

....

WRITER : HEMILKUMAR P PATEL

I am Hemilkumar P Patel. Who is mommy and daddy? The mother father of a son or daughter, So I want to send them a message. You people also take my point forward.

This is one of the things I wrote that I put in front of you in the form of a story. It happens that those who do timepass always break the heart of others and say that love like Krishna Radha. Understand that Krishna and Radha love each other, not like you, one playwright breaks one. They were both one. If Krishna is walking then the shadow falls on Radha and if Radha is walking then the shadow falls on Krishna. Boys and girls these days, when they say something good, they don't understand how badly they think about it. And the one who thinks good will leave it and that man will fight with himself all his life. For one thing, if you understand that a boy or a girl loves someone and does not appreciate others, then yes, what do you do? How sad it is to be released after saying yes, He/she will be in trouble for the rest of his/her life, You know that! By what right do you bother him? He/She does not force you to love, You break the heart of a man by passing the time, So let me tell you one thing, if you break someone's heart by playing a love game and passing the time, So you have no right to take true love. You have no right to be attached to it. You want to hurt him/her in the wrong way. If you can't make someone happy, do you have the right to hurt them? Put your hand on your heart and say to someone who has timepassed with someone, do you have the right to love him? Do you have the right to be with him? And when you are asked why you did timepass, So why do you answer MY LIFE MY RULES! I don't care if he/she dies! So you have no right to be in this world. If there is a player in drama, keep going. Every day there are vacancies in the drama company. There will be good employment in the drama company. If you don't understand the language of love, it will work, but if you don't play the move that makes the life of the person in front of hell. Answer me one thing, why did you say that you hate if you have made love? Where there is love there is no hatred, and where there is hatred love is never present.

This is my belief. Your belief can tell me. Thank you.

: HEMILKUMAR P PATEL

.